SO, YOU THINK YOU'RE A WRITER...

Other Books by Ian Gouge

Novels and Novellas

The Red Tie
17 Alma Road
Tilt
Once Significant Others
On Parliament Hill
A Pattern of Sorts
The Opposite of Remembering
At Maunston Quay
An Infinity of Mirrors
The Big Frog Theory
Losing Moby Dick and Other Stories

Short Story collections

Dust, dancing
An Irregular Piece of Sky
Degrees of Separation
Secrets & Wisdom

Poetry

Bound
Grimsby Docks
Crash
not the Sonnets
Selected Poems: 1976-2022
The Homelessness of a Child
The Myths of Native Trees
First-time Visions of Earth from Space
After the Rehearsals
Punctuations from History
Human Archaeology
Collected Poems (1979-2016)

Non-Fiction

Shrapnel from a Writing Life

Ian Gouge

So, you think you're a Writer…

First published in paperback by Coverstory books, 2024

ISBN 978-1-0686701-9-0

Copyright © Ian Gouge 2024

The right of Ian Gouge to be identified as the author of this work has been asserted by him in accordance with the Copyright, Designs and Patents Act 1988.

The cover image was built by the author utilising the Adobe suite of products © Ian Gouge 2024

All rights reserved.

No part of this publication may be reproduced, circulated, stored in a system from which it can be retrieved, or transmitted in any form without the prior permission of the publisher in writing.

www.iangouge.substack.com

www.iangouge.com

www.coverstorybooks.com

Contents

Introduction 3

Why do you write? 7
Who do you write for? 17
What kind of writer are you? 26
What are you writing? 34
"Tell me what the answer is…" 44
Persona / brand: does it matter? 48
The Challenge of Originality 57
Inspiration — or 'The Muse' 67
The Myth that is "Writer's Block" 73
Imposter Syndrome 85
'Planner' or 'Pantser'? 92
Planning - Z to A 98
The Importance of Character Profiles 106
Dialogue vs. Monologue 114
Poetry on the page 125
The Joy of Editing 134
Getting Published 146
Sundry Items
    Plotting 157
    Prose: long- or short-form 159
    Criticism / Critiquing 161
    The Role of Writing Groups & Open Mics 162
    Social Media 165
    Use of the Internet 166
    The Fickle World of Competitions 168
And finally, the 'quality' conundrum 170
So, are you a writer then? 178
Afterwords 183

Acknowledgements 191

INTRODUCTION

So, you think you're a writer?

Well, quite possibly you are. Indeed you may be a very good one. Or — and I suspect this is more likely — you tell yourself you're reasonably talented, but deep down you're not too sure...

Either that, or you are not as 'good' as you'd like to be.

Perhaps you don't know whether what you're trying to write is the thing you should be writing, or if you have the talent to carry it off; perhaps you're feeling disheartened by years of competition and Agent rejections and the underlying implications of such messages. Or maybe you're simply struggling to finish 'your novel'. Or even put pen to paper at all.

And what does a 'Writer' look like, anyway?

Common enough problems. I suspect the vast majority of writers will recognise at least one of them.

In order to rescue whatever it was that needing rescuing — or to locate whatever it was you were trying to find — you may well have tried courses, retreats. Perhaps you have delved into the myriad of 'How to' guides assuming they might provide the magic key to help unlock, well, everything.

After all, you're looking at this book, aren't you?

However, *So, you think you're a Writer* is a little different. It is not going to pretend there are secrets to be discovered, nor is it going to claim that there are 'right' answers. If someone tells you "this is how you write a novel" then be <u>*very*</u> sceptical.

The reason?

THERE ARE NO SECRETS, AND THERE ARE EVEN FEWER RIGHT ANSWERS!

If there were, we'd all be writing the same things and in the exactly the same ways... And we'd all be 'writers'.

But how do you define 'a writer' anyway? Most people write — even if it's just a shopping list! — so surely there must be some kind of 'qualification'.

Here are some dictionary definitions (with my <u>emphasis</u>):

- "a person who writes books or articles <u>to be published</u>" - Cambridge Dictionary (on-line)
- "a person engaged in writing books, articles, stories, etc., <u>especially as an occupation or profession</u>; an author or journalist" - dictionary.com
- "a writer is a person who writes books, stories, or articles <u>as a job</u>" - Collins Dictionary (on-line)

Clearly there are some issues with these definitions. If you equate "to be published" with "a job", then they suggest that only those who earn a living writing — or for whom writing is 'work' — are entitled to call themselves writers. On the one hand this certainly simplifies who can and who cannot be called 'a writer'. Indeed, faced with such a binary definition, it probably disqualifies the majority of those who regard themselves as writers. But what if you're writing full-time, perhaps a novel that is yet to be published? Or you've been writing short stories for twenty years? And what about poets and screenwriters and playwrights?

Yet if you relax the definition there's a problem too. If Sam has written two poems does that make them a writer? What about if they've written ten? Or fifty? Where's the threshold they need to cross in order to qualify — and who's to say anyway? The spectre of publication as arbiter raises its head again, and then we are back full circle to the dictionary definitions.

This conundrum is one of the reasons that the assertion "I am a writer" is far more problematic than you might imagine, and as such validates the need to go deeper into what it means to be 'a writer'.

In this book there are many more questions than answers — and those questions are aimed squarely at you. Consequently there is work involved. Yes, there will be some suggestions along the way, but at the heart of the book lays an objective to peel back the veneer we apply to ourselves when we choose to believe "I am a writer". This self-examination should not only reveal how robust that veneer is, but whether it has any substance at all. This is not for my benefit, but for yours; an opportunity for you to take an honest look at yourself — at your writing persona — and not only validate it, but to see if it's providing you with the best possible foundation to succeed.

To do so, the book adopts a starting position which effectively says "you tell me that you're a writer, but I'm not sure I believe you". The premise is that simply because if you *say* you're one thing or another doesn't necessarily mean that you are... Many people will disagree, of course; they will have their own beliefs, self-confidence, faith, whatever. And that's fine.

But irrespective of that, do you know if you are living your 'best' writing life? Are you maximising what you could achieve?

Of course you could simply carry on as you do now, settling for the easy life of the regular writing prompt, the "that's nice, dear" feedback from your local writing group, the unpublished manuscripts, the rejected submissions, and *never* ask the hard questions, never rise to the challenges these present. And you can continue to hope that doing tomorrow what you're doing today — ignoring the why, what and how of it — may one day deliver a different result.

Isn't that a definition of insanity?

Personally I have been there, suffered the doubts, faced the interminable questions: "what is *this*?", "is it good enough?", "am I writing what I'm *supposed* to write?", "what's the point?", "am I 'a writer' anyway?" It has taken many years — and many hundreds of thousands of words — to reach conclusions with which I'm satisfied. For now, at least. In many respects this book represents a distillation of decades of trial and error, of lessons learned the hard way — and those gleaned from other writers. There will be theories, proposals, views with which you may not agree, and that's just fine. As I said, no right answers…

Whichever way you approach it, the writing journey can be a painful one — maybe it *should* be a painful one — therefore if I can help you just a little, then that's good enough for me.

So if you're up for the challenge of taking an honest look at 'you-as-writer', then please read on…

Ian Gouge, 2024

WHY DO YOU WRITE?

As a creative writing mentor I am often asked the 'right way' of doing something, especially when people have a preconceived idea in terms of what it is they *have* to write. The latter is most commonly evidenced in people who believe they <u>must</u> write a novel. If they don't, how can they possibly call themselves 'a writer'…?

Shakespeare never wrote a novel; nor did Milton, Dylan Thomas, Yeats — but you wouldn't deny they were writers, would you?

Trying to divine the 'correct way' to execute our craft is to put the proverbial cart before the horse — especially as there are more fundamental things a writer needs resolve.

THE FIRST CHALLENGES YOU SHOULD ADDRESS ARE NOT OUTWARDS TOWARDS YOUR WORK, BUT INWARDS TOWARD YOURSELF

For me there are three fundamental questions that need to be posed *before* you go on to examine what you are writing. Indeed, tackling these questions and coming to an honest appraisal of who you are as a writer — often in relation to specific projects, as we shall see — is fundamental. After all, would you build a house without foundations?

Many tutors and coaches, or those who offer assistance either in-person or on-line, often retreat to the safety of 'aids' like writing prompts. Their goal in doing so is to get you writing, and to keep you writing. Laudable of course, but the problem with things like writing prompts is that they can actually mask your underlying issue and therefore hinder your tackling it.

Similarly, you often see homogenous and vacuous advice suggesting that, if you do X, Y and Z, acceptance from an Agent *will* come, your book *will* make it into print, you *will* be successful.

Whilst I understand the motivational intentions behind such messages, they are fundamentally dishonest.

And it's worse than that.

THE VAST MAJORITY OF WRITERS WILL NEVER CREATE SOMETHING OF SUFFICIENT QUALITY OR COMMERCIAL INTEREST TO BE PUBLISHED VIA THE TRADITIONAL ROUTE

We'll talk about publishing and prompts and inspiration later on, but for now think on this: take on-board all the prompts you want, absorb all those inspirational quotes you find littering social media, yet none of these will, in and of themselves, turn you into a good writer. How can they?

Surely the starting block for any writer who is serious about their craft is more fundamental than internet-delivered superficiality. Indeed, my key question is this: **how can you ever fulfil the potential you may have if you do not understand yourself and your relationship to your work?**

I could take a piece of wood, go into my garage, and hack at it with some chisels. Would that qualify me to call myself 'a sculptor'? Of course not! That would be ridiculous. I would need practice, training in the craft, accumulation of skills — yet at the end of the day that would guarantee nothing. It takes something else, something 'extra'. I am confident that no matter how dedicated I was, I would never be able to legitimately call myself 'a sculptor'. I have taken thousands of photographs but do not consider myself 'a photographer'; painted many pictures, but am not 'a painter'. To make such claims would be an insult to photographers and painters!

Yet as soon as we put a few words together, draft a couple of poems, we are more than happy to call ourselves 'writers', often doing so without suffering the pains of practice, of working at the craft. And, it must be said, sometimes without the prerequisite skills too.

Just because you call yourself 'a writer' doesn't mean you are one.

I once met a man who had just written his first poem and because, when he read it aloud, no-one gave him honest feedback, he wondered if he could now call himself 'a poet'…

Similarly, having a formal qualification — like a creative writing degree — means nothing other than proving you have the ability to attend the relevant course and go through an academic process. I have met people with such a qualification who had no idea about rhythm or tempo; much of their work was bereft of quality.

Which would be exactly the same when it came to my theoretical sculpting of wood. Beyond a lack of practice, skills and talent, my fundamental problems would be that I didn't know *why* I was trying to sculpt, nor who I was doing it for. Indeed, I might not even be able to articulate what I was trying to create!

Therefore, why should other creative pursuits be any different?

Not only do the majority of us fail to recognise these somewhat 'existential' questions, when we do we rarely pose them to ourselves. And why is that? Because they're difficult? Because we think them irrelevant? Because we have never even thought to challenge ourselves with them? Or because we are happy to label what we do as 'Art', quote inspiration and 'The Muse', and leave it at that?

WE <u>SHOULD</u> ASK OURSELVES THOSE HARD QUESTIONS;
THEY ARE THE WAY-MARKERS TO WHICH WE MUST RETURN
AGAIN AND AGAIN THROUGHOUT OUR WRITING LIVES

And why continually return to them? Because the answers can change over time depending on personal circumstance and/or what you are trying to write. Indeed, how you answer them can help inform what you should or should not be writing.

So, to start this journey in earnest, let's tackle 'the biggie'…

QUESTION 1: WHY DO YOU WRITE?

Have you ever really asked yourself this — and done so seriously and honestly?

Most writers write because it's something they've always done, or because writing takes them to their 'happy place'. But there are many, many more answers to the question, and most of these are far less superficial or 'easy'. On its own, this simple fact validates the notion that when it comes to writing there is no universally 'right' answer. How can there be? We are individuals, come to writing with differing backgrounds and experiences, with various aspirations perhaps. And we're all writing different things.

'A novel' is a pretty meaningless construct when explaining what you are trying to write. Even sub-defining it into genres does little to recognise uniqueness. And 'poetry' is not one thing; it's a complex panoply of possibilities. All of which is one of the reasons I avoid 'How To' books; if it was that easy, we'd all be doing it.

THE OUTPUT OF GOOD WRITING IS NOT A COMMODITY

So, back to the question: **why do you write**?

What is it that drives you to sit down and spend your precious time stringing words together, irrespective of genre, whether poetry or prose or screenplay, fiction or non-fiction etc.?

Hint: "because I'm a writer" is <u>not</u> an acceptable answer! And if that was indeed your instinctive response, then that demonstrates you have never actively considered the 'why' question...

So here are a few possible answers, some of which may resonate with you:

Because it passes the time

Undoubtedly true. But then so does gardening, knitting, taking long walks. I would argue that 'passing the time' is more the by-product of a hobby. Yet if that is *honestly* why you write — for that and for no other reason — then fair enough. Remember, there is no 'right' answer, only the answer that best fits you.

Because it's your job

This may require further definition I suppose, but the criteria *could* be that writing is what you get paid to do, and you have no other income. It is your 'work'. One nuance is that you may indeed be approaching writing as work but are not yet reaping any reward from it, financial or otherwise i.e. there is zero income and thus far you may have no concrete output, no meaningful reviews. Under such circumstances, it may still be valid to regard writing as 'a job'.

Because you can't help it

Compulsion. Addiction. You choose the word. There are those writers who simply can't stop themselves: they *must* write that next short story, that next poem; they cannot stem the flow of ideas, the things about which they have no choice but to compile chains of words. And that's irrespective of the quality of their output. [The notion of 'quality' and how that validates or undermines one's status as a writer is a very thorny issue, and one to which we will return later.]

Because writing helps you make sense of the world

You only have to think back to Covid-19. The world was suddenly awash with poems about the pandemic; people found themselves compelled to write 'their Covid poem'. If most of these weren't very good, in a way that didn't matter; the poem was the writer's way of *processing* the situation. For many the same is true of Ukraine or Gaza. And on an individual level, people may use writing to make sense of their own circumstances: the death of a loved one; their sexuality; a domestic crisis; their past. Perhaps this is one of the sources of memoir.

Because it's therapeutic

Another flavour of the reason above, but where the goal is to make yourself feel better in some way. Writing — and its output — can improve your self-esteem, how you feel abut your place in the world; it can act as a salve, self-medication almost. And the boost offered can come not just from working something through, the process of writing, but in terms of the kick you get when something is finished, or via the feedback received.

Because you want to be published

Publication *may* be little more than a badge of honour. Perhaps you feel that the only way to validate that you're 'a writer' is to get something into print. After all, what more proof do you need? However, getting published via a conventional route isn't easy. And self-publishing? Many people take their one manuscript, utilise Amazon Kindle

Direct to create a Kindle book and hey presto! There they are on Amazon. Technology has gifted us democratisation; anyone can publish a book. But self-publishing is a double-edge sword. There is no quality control. Just having an ebook available on Amazon doesn't make it 'good' — and depending on how you make the assessment, lack of quality in your ebook may disqualify you as 'a writer' in any event.

Because you want to make money

Based on recent surveys in the UK, the average income for people identifying as writers is somewhat less than £10k per annum (c. $12k). If you take away the very few who make a great deal, then perhaps the 'average writer' earns not much more than £7k. Therefore, if you want to make money there are easier — and more reliable — ways to do so! Make no mistake though, this can still be a valid reason to be a writer and — perhaps more than any other — this 'why' can have a very real and direct bearing on the 'what' of your work.

Because you want to be famous

It seems these days that the natural sequence of events is to become famous *then* write a book. The industry loves celebrity authors in part because publishers' commercial risks are significantly reduced. Celebrity sells. A celebrity could write the worst book in the world and it be a publishing success — and some of us might think we can point to such examples. Very few writers — people who do nothing but write — are truly 'famous'. How many can you name? And often this fame comes not directly from their books but from spin-offs like film or television adaptations. Being famous can still be your motivation to write, but you might be better served by applying to be on 'reality tv'…

Because you want to leave a legacy

> Even if we shy away from it, we all know that one day we're not going to be around any more. You might be aiming to provide a legacy for your family, your children and grandchildren. This knowledge is enough for many people to put pen to paper, their goal being to leave something of themselves behind, often memoir.

These are just a few of the obvious answers to the question 'why do you write'; undoubtedly there are many more. If none from the list above strikes you as being 'true', then I suggest you need to uncover your personal motivation.

DEFINING THE CORE REASON BEHIND WHY WE WRITE IS ABSOLUTELY FUNDAMENTAL IN UNDERSTANDING OUR AUTHORIAL MAKE-UP

And this is important because?

Well, soon we are going to look at two further fundamental questions about being a writer: deciding who we are writing for, and recognising what kind of writer we are. In order to get the best out of ourselves — the most 'success' in terms of our output both in 'what' we write *and* to achieve greater authenticity as 'a writer' — the answers to all three of these questions *must* be in harmony.

A trivial example. Let's say you are crystal clear that you write in order to make money, and for no other reason. A perfectly valid answer. But against that motivation, if all you write are limericks or poetry, or fillers for your local newspaper, then it is highly likely that what you are producing will *never* satisfy your reason for writing. The 'why' and the 'what' of your writing will be out of alignment — and alignment of your fundamentals is key to you becoming the best and most contented writer possible. Either the 'why' or 'what' needs to change.

IN ORDER TO BE THE MOST EFFECTIVE AND HAPPY WRITER YOU CAN BE, YOU NEED TO BE UNDERTAKING THE PROJECTS WHICH FIT YOU AS AN INDIVIDUAL – AND THE ROUTE TO DEFINING THOSE IS TO HONESTLY CHALLENGE YOUR UNDERSTANDING OF YOURSELF

THE QUESTIONS YOU NEED TO ASK YOURSELF...

In this instance, there is just one: "Why do you write?"

You need to engage the question seriously and come up with an honest assessment, one you *know* to be true — not one you think is 'right' or expected of you. Nor one you've settled on just to enable you to go on to the next chapter.

Truthfully, why do you write?

Imagine yourself going into an interview; the role you have applied for is 'Writer'. "Why do you write?" is going to be the first question you are asked. Not only do you need to believe in your answer, you need to convince the interviewer that you are being honest, sincere, genuine, self-aware.

And the same will be true of later questions too.

...AND THINGS TO TRY

Concerned you may have settled on something too easily? Or that your answer is little more than what might be considered conventional? That if challenged further, you may not be able to provide the evidence needed? Then take your answer for a spin.

Pick something you have previously written — or are in the process of writing — and ask yourself whether the 'why' you have arrived at feels appropriate *as justification for that work*. In the main, it should. "I'm writing my memoir because I want to leave a legacy"; tick, that fits. But "I'm writing poetry because I want to be rich and famous"; I hardly think so.

But be aware, it may be entirely legitimate for there to be discrepancies. "I wrote A because of X, but I'm writing B because of Y." This is perfectly acceptable — provided A & X and B & Y are in harmony. Remember what I said about revisiting these questions regularly, and how your answers may change based on what you're working on, circumstances etcetera?

If you have settled on the core reason for why you write, then soon enough you should be able to pass judgement on yourself i.e. not only whether you really are a writer, but on what basis you make that assessment.

WHO DO YOU WRITE FOR?

Thus far we have looked at the first of three fundamental questions you need to ask yourself before you can go on to analyse whether what you are writing is appropriate for the kind of writer you are — and to begin validation that you are 'a writer' at all.

That initial question was **Why do you write?**

Did you try to answer it, and if you did so — being ruthlessly honest of course! — were you surprised by the answer? You probably weren't, though that may change later...

However, if you chose not to, or settled on a motivation which is at best superficial, then I encourage you to try again. Without having the solid foundation of understanding *why* you write, you will lose the benefit of the triangulation and insight to which such knowledge can contribute.

Assuming you're comfortable that you write for legacy or money or because of addiction etcetera, now is the time to consider the second question:

QUESTION 2: WHO DO YOU WRITE FOR?

This is another poser which might initially appear somewhat rudimentary. The most common answer — especially amongst those for whom writing is a non-professional endeavour — is likely to be that "I write for myself", which is an entirely acceptable response. And as with 'why do you write', there aren't going to be any wrong answers.

Yet if you give yourself some time to really think about this second question, you may find that landing on the most appropriate response is far less cut-and-dried than you first assumed.

Here are some possible (and plausible) answers — though perhaps not all of them would be valid if you were to adhere to the dictionary definitions we saw in the previous chapter (i.e. writer as 'professional'):

I write for myself

You might well argue that not only is this likely to be the most popular response, it will *always* be at least part of the answer i.e. you may be writing for someone special, but you are *also* writing for yourself. Indeed, in some senses how can you not be? Yet while this may be true, there is something profound about being the *only* person for whom you are writing, which is what this answer implies. There is just one person to satisfy: yourself. Potentially just one person who will pass judgement.

Are you saying, for example, that you are your only reader?

'I write for myself' also places you on a continuum where at one end you may never be satisfied with your work, and at the other you are only too happy to bask in self-anointed glory — or get away with literary murder! The extremes are likely to be marked by your declaiming "everything I write is rubbish!" or "that's simply flawless!"

Where you sit on this spectrum is important in your assessment of self. If you are never satisfied with your work then you are less likely to regard yourself as a writer (when you may be a perfectly capable one); and if you are narcissistic, then "I am a writer" will come all too easily — even if you're not a very good one.

Or not one at all.

I write for someone special

There are obvious examples of output driven by such motivation: love poems, eulogies, often children's stories. If you could ask Tolkien for whom he was writing *Lord of the Rings*, he'd probably tell you that it was his son. I suspect Raynor Winn's *The Salt Path* was at least partly written for her husband. And Shakespeare's *Sonnets*? Indeed, in the context of this question it could be instructive to consider anything ever published and try to imagine for whom it was written.

One of the differences with 'I write for someone special' is that the motivation might be transitory — love is fickle after all! — or it might be tied to a particular project. If Shakespeare wrote some of *The Sonnets* for 'The Dark Lady', he most certainly would not have penned *Coriolanus* for her! A different 'who' based on the 'what'. Or vice versa.

I write for other people / 'my readers'

If I am wary of this as an answer to the question 'who do you write for' it is because — as with 'I write for myself' — it has the potential to be something of a 'cop out'. The risk is that we talk of 'our readers' in a glib, offhand, or even slightly superior way. Some writers try to have a specific reader in mind, almost as if they are writing for 'someone special'; indeed, in some cases they may be one and the same person.

When it comes to 'readers', the notion of a reading community can be closely tied to what you are writing. For example, in genre fiction — murder-mystery or sci-fi, for example — the tribes likely to read your work may be relatively easy to define. The most extreme example of an understood and specifically written-for community is probably that served by Mills & Boon romances where the audience is so well known that the books written to a strict formula.

So, if you believe that you write for 'your readers' or an 'ideal' reader or an 'audience', I would encourage you to try and define them. Age, sex, socio-economic factors, interests and so forth. Are they lawyers, students, members of Hell's Angels, nurses, train drivers, children? Readers are people too, and not an amorphous mass. Having a clear idea of your target recipient(s) may help you validate not only whether you are writing the right thing for them, but also *how* you are approaching it (in terms of style etc.). It may also give you the opportunity to look back at yourself from their perspective and ask whether or not *they* would consider *you* 'a writer'...

I write for the Bank Manager / my Publisher

This may be partly tongue-in-cheek (the Bank Manager suggestion at least!) yet we do need to acknowledge that the 'who' we are writing for may be a 'virtual' or commercial entity i.e. we write to satisfy someone else — and not necessarily in the intellectual or emotional sense.

We all have bills to pay and if your writing offers you a way of meeting financial commitments then — notions of readers aside — there is a commercial imperative in play. The same is true if you have a contract for a project, a deadline to hit. You can tell yourself that you're writing for yourself or your readers, but there is a spectre sitting on your shoulder demanding to be satisfied.

And why is this significant? Because it can really 'mess with your head' a) if you're not used to it, and b) if you fail to recognise it. I'll offer a real example of this in a later chapter.

AT THE END OF THE DAY, WHAT YOUR READERS THINK OF YOU IS THE MOST IMPORTANT ASSESSMENT OF ALL

I think it not unreasonable to suggest that, over the course of their endeavours, writers may go on some kind of journey in terms of who they are writing for. Was Dickens writing for himself or his readers — or to meet the deadlines of *The Strand Magazine*? How much might that have changed over time? What about JKRowling: did the 'who' she was writing for gradually shift? Were the drivers behind *The Deathly Hallows* subtly different to those for *The Philosopher's Stone*? I'm not saying they were, but you can see how they might have been.

Given how personal the 'who' can be, undoubtedly there are more potential answers than the four suggested above — though probably not as many as for the 'why' question; after all, the target recipient for your work should be identifiable.

Check the list again. Can you think of others for whom you could be writing? Still sticking with the first answer you thought of?

WHY DOES THIS MATTER?

As I said previously, when it comes to these fundamental questions it's all about alignment. As writers, we need to get ourselves into a space where the answers to 'why do you write?' and 'who do you write for?' — as well as the forthcoming third question — are in harmony with each other. If you can achieve this, not only will you have laid a firm foundation upon which to build your work, but you will be better placed to confirm whether or not you can call yourself a writer.

Remember our interview scenario? Let's assume — perhaps after a little further interrogation — that the interviewer was happy enough with your response to the 'why' question. Now you also have to convince them of the authenticity of your 'who' answer. They will be checking to see if you are contradicting yourself, trying to identify any conflict between the two.

For example, if in response to 'why' you said you are writing to make sense of your life, but for 'who' declared you were writing for a specific audience — let's say children, just to illustrate the point. It is fairly obvious that those two answers are incompatible i.e. your target audience is probably not the least bit interested in your life. And potentially vice versa: you may not be that committed to writing something that will captivate children. However, if your answer to 'why' was that you wrote to share your deep knowledge of a specific subject — Tort law, for example — then that would align incredibly well if your target audience was lawyers. If you said you wrote in order to fulfil a contract and thus were writing for your publisher, those answers would also be aligned wouldn't they? How could an interviewer not be impressed?

You get the point.

However — and this is key — when tackling who you write for, try and approach it in isolation

I know it will be hard to separate the second challenge from the first, but it is very easy to 'cross-contaminate' answers and come up with a 'pat' combination where your 'who' is a perfect match for the 'why' on which you have already settled. Arrived at consciously or subconsciously, under such circumstances your responses may be 'neat' but possibly not a true reflection of you at all.

Honesty — ruthless honesty — is the critical thing, especially if you want to be serious about understanding your motivation, alignment, and the rest.

UNSUBSTANTIATED OFF-PAT ANSWERS WON'T CUT THE MUSTARD

Once you have landed on a 'why' and 'who' with which you're happy, then you should validate these by looking in the rear-view mirror. Such validation can be invaluable.

For example, let's say you said you are writing for yourself, and this aligns with why you write. You may be happy with those answers, but are they potentially a little 'thin'? Would you concede that you might be applying some cheap and low-grade veneer to your endeavours? So consider what you really mean by 'writing for yourself'. Are you pursuing a desire to increase your self-esteem? To revel in the satisfaction of hitting targets like word counts or hours writing per day? Or to prove to yourself that you can set your mind to something and follow it through? All of these are perfectly respectable sub-categories of 'writing for yourself'; each has a different slant, may be closer to the 'real' answer, and as a result may align much better with your 'why'.

ANSWERS TO THE KEY QUESTIONS CAN ALMOST ALWAYS BE REFINED

Later, when you have your met the third challenge and we move on to consider *what* you are actually writing, we can undertake a sense-check from both directions; we will work forward from the 'why', through the 'who' etc. towards the 'what', and then back the other way. This is the triangulation to which I referred earlier.

So, you may now think you know why you write and who you are writing for — but ask yourself, is the interviewer impressed? If you stood up in front of a group of peers at a writing retreat and gave them your story, would they find it credible and authentic?

THE QUESTIONS YOU NEED TO ASK YOURSELF...

Having arrived at a response to who you write for, challenge yourself:

Does someone who professes such an ambition really sound like you?

> Deep down, you might know yourself to be an entirely selfish individual and therefore to say you are writing for others... well, it doesn't ring true, does it?

If a friend or writing acquaintance was asked to answer the 'who' question on your behalf, would they reach the same conclusion?

> And if your 'who' is a real person — a friend or relative, say — would they recognise that what you were writing or had written was for them? Again, this is to tackle head-on the possibility that you are trying to kid yourself. What would 'The Dark Lady' have said about Shakespeare and *The Sonnets* — especially if she suspected that a chunk of them were written to a man?

If the why-who combination you have landed on is a good fit, ask yourself if you arrived at it more from a desire to be 'neat' than to be accurate.

> If the two options you have chosen were suddenly disallowed, what would your alternatives look like and how well do *they* align? And if you consider them a fallback (i.e. to give you a first and second choice for both 'why' and 'who') is there a different combination which describes you better?

...AND THINGS TO TRY

Again you can challenge your notion of who you are writing for by looking at current works-in-progress or things you have previously written. Who do you think those pieces are written for, and does that knowledge fit with the answer at which you previously arrived?

Of course you can legitimately find more than one 'who' rising from the ashes of past endeavours. If some do not fit who you thought they were for, then ask yourself why not? If none of them do, then you need to seriously re-evaluate who is the target for your writing, because either your original assessment was flawed or you have been misleading yourself. Perhaps you went with convenient or logical options and now have demonstrated their inaccuracy.

I THINK THE 'WHO' REQUIRING THE GREATEST CHALLENGE IS THE BLAND "I WRITE FOR MYSELF"

Different genres of writing will lean toward different answers, too. A volume of poetry, for example, may contain a number of love poems, eulogies, poems about events from your past, or the major concerns of the present day. In a single collection there could be multiple 'who's', so in such a case think about the collection as a whole. Poetry may, in general, lean toward the self-indulgent; fiction toward a reader community; plays and screenplays towards satisfying an audience in 'real time'; non-fiction the sharing of knowledge with readers.

WHATEVER YOU ARE WRITING, NEVER ASSUME THE OBVIOUS 'WHO' IS THE ONLY ANSWER

It may well be that at this stage you have arrived at an interim conclusion which suggests that there are one or two reasons why you write — and multiple answers to the question as to who all this writing is for. If so, when we come to examine the 'what' of your writing in a couple of chapters time, the fog should lift.

But having said that, please don't use that promise as a stay of execution, an excuse not to try and distill your answers now.

WHAT KIND OF WRITER ARE YOU?

So far we've looked at two of the fundamental questions you need to ask yourself in order to garner creative context *before* you go on to consider what you are writing, and indeed whether you should be writing that particular thing at all.

Hopefully you have attempted to resolve why you write and who you write for, and tried to validate that they are in alignment — and if not, understood where the disconnect might be. The outcome — even if your answers are slightly out of true — may not require you to do very much at this stage because it takes all these exercises combined to help you gain a better understanding of your 'writing self'.

The third question is, as they say, 'different gravy'. Given this one is about process, it is one whose answer may very well result in a call-to-action…

QUESTION 3: WHAT KIND OF WRITER ARE YOU?

When we sit down to write it seems logical that we should know why we are doing so and who we're writing for. Of course there are likely to be times when we simply 'go with the flow', but even then we should be able to tag our activity with a very clear understanding of the 'why' and the 'who'. Some people — 'pantsers' — can take this to an extreme, working without any kind of schema or plan, not knowing if the piece they are working on will be a short story, a novella, or a novel. Which is all fine; we'll look at pantsers vs. planners later on.

The third question in our base triumvirate is, however, aligned to the mechanics of your writing process.

For example, you might identify with one of these:

Are you structured & disciplined, a 9-to-5 kind of writer?

Perhaps you like to set aside a particular time of day or day of the week to write; or perhaps you need a target — words or hours — to hit every time you put pen to paper. These are the traits of a structured writer. The approach adopted in the *process* of writing is critical to you, and if you are unable to hit your writing slot or fail to meet your regular target you can't help but feel negative, perhaps sensing that you have let yourself — and your writing — down.

There are numerous examples of writers who confess to needing such a regime: so many words a day no matter how long that might take, or a certain amount of time irrespective of the nature and quality of the output — for example, a routine of starting writing at a set hour each morning and continuing until 1,500 words have been drafted. There are many similar examples from across the decades.[1]

It is worth noting that the majority of writers who pursue such a strict regime are likely to be middle-aged men, one way or another freed from the demands of domesticity. It is harder for women to adhere to a rigid process given what society — and men in particular — demand of them in terms of their roles as wives and mothers.

Hopefully this is now changing.

---

[1] see *Daily Rituals: How Artists Work*, Mason Currey (2013) plus later 2020 editions

Do you 'go-with-the-flow'?

At the other extreme is the person who is happy to write when the mood takes them, who remains unencumbered by set times or targets. Not writing for a week or a month is no issue — and sitting down and writing for seven straight hours is no big deal either. "It's just the way things are; 'life' gets in the way". But be aware, this is not the same as being 'a pantser'. A pantser's lack of planning is more focussed on *what* they write; they may still like to have the discipline of a thousand words a day, it is simply that they have no idea what those thousand words will be about.

Are you methodical?

This isn't about time or targets (though they're not mutually exclusive), but relates to the process of how you put words down on paper. For example, you may draft something on Day One then begin Day Two with a quick edit of the previous day's effort before pushing on. Day Three begins with editing what you'd drafted on Day Two before you pen some more. And so on. Eventually there will come a designated point when you review everything together.

Or perhaps you start your writing session with an exercise — a very short piece of flash fiction or a haiku perhaps — just to get the creative juices flowing. Or you have a routine which involves reading aloud what you have written.

Your method is essentially that A is followed by B, and B is followed by C; what A, B and C are is entirely down to you — but you seldom waiver from that sequence.

Are you a reluctant writer?

This is an interesting one. It is often categorised as someone who desperately wants to write, but allows themselves to be constantly distracted by other things — cleaning, cooking, walking the dog — in order to *avoid* writing. Or, knowing they need 'help', they have tried various forms of targets, goal-setting, reservations of time etc. to see if any of those gives them the discipline to write. Often none of that works.

The reluctant writer is neither disciplined nor structured, nor are they casual or methodical. They are not 'blocked' either. They are very clear what they wish to write about, they simply find the process of <u>starting</u> *hard*.

Are you an obsessive?

Do you write all the time? On buses, in coffee shops, in the bathroom, during the adverts on TV? Do you carry a notebook wherever you go, or locate them strategically around the house? Obsessive writers can be a little like the casual writer in that they may not work to a defined schedule — but they are at the other end of the spectrum in that they can't stop!

I suspect it may be fear and certainty that drives the obsessive: the fear that they may suddenly have a great idea and are afraid of losing it (hence all the notepads!), and the certainty that their Muse can strike at any time and so they want to be constantly 'at work' in order to give it maximum opportunities to pay a visit.

Undoubtedly there will be more 'types' of writer than the rudimentary few listed above. In the vast majority of cases the category into which you fall will be a reflection on how you are made, your psychological profile, a manifestation of some subconscious preference or other. More than that, you may define yourself as an amalgam of various traits. I am not a total obsessive, but I do keep a notepad in the bathroom in case words start writing themselves in the middle of the night…

INDEED, AS WITH 'WHY' AND 'WHO', SOME BLEND MAY FIT YOU BEST – AND THAT'S FINE

Although I've suggested that you might be an X or a Y or a Z, hopefully you can appreciate that defining what it is to be a writer isn't straightforward — it's as awkward as those dictionary definitions are inadequate! Our theoretical interviewer may have provided us with a job description against which we can be measured, but like all jobs the reality of it will be different to what's written on the spec.

And how are you doing in your interview, by the way?

Unlike the 'why' and 'who' of our general conundrum, the difference with the 'type' response is that you can experiment, try things out. Unhappy being a casual writer? Try working to a schedule. Feeling tied down by your goals and targets? What happens when you throw them away for a while? Do you feel liberated? Is your work freer, more enjoyable?

Having said that, as with the answers to the previous two questions, alignment is the critical factor.

For example, if your 'why' and 'who' are perfectly aligned in that you are writing for a publisher in order to meet a contract (with all the attendant commitments to dates etc.), you can immediately see how being a 'go-with-the-flow' or 'casual' writer might be problematic: the likelihood is that you are not going to fare very well in hitting dates. You might say the same if you were a 'reluctant' writer, too. Yet in recognising as much, you could potentially put a regime in place which might help you address that i.e. to start heading towards the 'methodical'. Someone who is structured and disciplined will have far less trouble in hitting deadlines.

Alternatively — putting the 'why' and 'who' aside — by nature you might be a 'structured' kind of individual, but your lifestyle (work, family etc.) may prevent you from adhering to a rigid schedule no matter how hard you try. If so, this could prove frustrating. In order to be more satisfied/creative/productive you may therefore need to educate yourself to be relaxed about when and how you write, give yourself permission to miss a writing slot or two.

THE 'KIND' OF PROCESS PERSON YOU ARE IS MOST SIGNIFICANT WHEN CONSIDERED AGAINST WHAT YOU ARE WRITING

Do not underestimate the value in holding up this particular mirror to yourself. For example, if you are an unstructured pantser there will be things you could write for which such an approach is best suited. Having said that, I once came across a pantser who wrote complex murder mysteries with no forethought at all. I would have imagined such a genre — perhaps more than most — demanded decent planning and plotting to produce a credible and coherent end-product...

As with the previous two questions, there are no 'wrong' answers to the 'type' question — but there will most definitely be sub-optimal combinations.

So, you should now have answers to three questions: Why do you write? Who do you write for? What kind of writer are you?

Are you happy with your answers? Do they truly reflect you? You should be able to look at them and recognise yourself; and your erstwhile interviewer should have reached this stage of the process believing the responses their candidate is giving them — though that's not yet the same as successfully landing the job!

In the next chapter we will examine why all this is important — especially when considering 'what' you are writing…

The questions you need to ask yourself…

When you look back at your previous work can you remember which felt the most rewarding, which were easiest to write, progressed smoothly? If so, what approach did you take at the time — casual, structured etc. — and how well did that fit with both your life constraints and what you were trying to produce?

Similarly, what about the projects you found most difficult — perhaps even abandoned? How much was the process you were following responsible for that difficulty?

In my mentoring work I have often found that when writers are struggling with an aspect of their work, they often know where the issue lies. Subconsciously, they can see a way through it; all they need is some help to articulate that. Looking back at what you have produced or are working on, and understanding what went well (or otherwise), can give you a real insight into 'why', 'who' and 'type'. For example, did you find it difficult to motivate yourself when you were trying to use writing as therapy? Or find it impossible to focus when working on something overtly political? Or lose focus without having a plan or schedule to work to?

> THERE ARE VALUABLE LESSONS TO BE LEARNED FROM PRIOR EXPERIENCE – THOUGH TOO OFTEN WE IGNORE THEM!

…And things to try

If you have a work-in-progress you are trying to bring to a successful conclusion, try mapping out the remainder of the work in sufficient detail — chapter by chapter, poem by poem etc. — and break that down in a variety of ways: words per day/week; hours per day/week; chapters/poems (sic) per day/week etcetera. Which of these feels the most comfortable, suggests itself as being the most achievable? And keep it realistic! Then try that approach — especially if you don't normally work that way.

Again in consideration of current projects, do you like working on one thing at a time or do you need multiple things on the go? If you are struggling to make meaningful progress on one project, try the opposite i.e. multiple projects if you are used to working on only one. Or only one project if you are used to working on many. Remember, there is no 'right' answer, only appropriate ones based on circumstance and experience.

I always have more than one project on the go at any one time. This only changes when I'm about 80% through something; at that point I often give that project maximum focus in order to get it over the line as quickly as possible — then I go back to multiple endeavours. I have arrived at this process thanks to years of trial and error and experimentation, learning what does and doesn't work for me.

Experience is vital not only in understanding what type of writer you are, but also the 'why' and 'who' of your profile.

TRY NEW THINGS BY ALL MEANS, BUT NEVER LOSE THE LESSONS OF THE PAST

WHAT ARE YOU WRITING?

If you have stayed with me over the previous chapters hopefully you will have begun to answer three key questions:

Why do you write?

Who do you write for?

What kind of writer are you?

In doing so perhaps you have been able to appreciate where your answers are in harmony — and where they may not be. As I have said before, alignment is key.

And now the fourth question:

QUESTION 4: WHAT ARE YOU WRITING?

You might imagine the winning post is now in sight, that you are about to find out whether you can indeed call yourself a writer. Well, not quite yet... And if you expect this final poser to be nothing more than a formality, be warned; it may not be. Indeed, you might be slightly nervous about it if your previous answers have occasionally felt somehow out-of-kilter.

The good news is that how you answer this last question *may* help all the pieces fall into place.

THIS ONE IS THE EASIEST QUESTION TO ANSWER QUICKLY – BUT BEING 'EASY' DOESN'T MEAN YOUR ANSWER WILL BE 'RIGHT'...

How to start? Just take a look on your desk, in your notebooks, at the files on your computer. Somewhere there will be tangible evidence of the project (or projects) you are working on; and, after the more nebulous topics we've already tackled, surely they represent — finally! — entities that are open to concrete definition. For example [all definitions taken from Wikipedia]:

a novel or novella

"A novel is an extended work of narrative fiction usually written in prose and published as a book."

"A novella is a narrative prose fiction whose length is shorter than most novels, but longer than most short stories."

some short stories or flash fiction

"A short story is a piece of prose fiction that can typically be read in a single sitting and focuses on a self-contained incident or series of linked incidents, with the intent of evoking a single effect or mood."

"Flash fiction is a brief fictional narrative that still offers character and plot development... defined by word count."

a collection of poems

"Poetry is a form of literature that uses aesthetic and often rhythmic qualities of language — such as phonaesthetics, sound symbolism, and metre — to evoke meanings in addition to, or in place of, a prosaic ostensible meaning."

some non-fiction

"Non-fiction is any document or media content that attempts, in good faith, to convey information only about the real world, rather than being grounded in imagination."

drama i.e. a play or screenplay

"Drama is the specific mode of fiction represented in performance: a play, opera, mime, ballet, etc., performed in a theatre, or on radio or television or cinema."

Simple, yes?

Well, not quite. For example, one of the most common questions I hear people ask is "How long is a novel / novella / short story?"

Given 'long', 'medium', and 'short' won't satisfy you — "give me numbers!" — you might argue that novels are 60k words or more, short stories 15k words or less, and novellas everything in between. But these days that's 'old-school' given there are many commercially successful novels that come in at well under sixty-thousand words.

IN ANY EVENT, THE LENGTH OF YOUR PIECE OF FICTION IS TOTALLY IRRELEVANT

Size has nothing whatsoever to do with the merit of what you're producing — nor does one thing or the other automatically 'qualify' you as 'a writer'.

Okay, so you're writing a novel — perhaps largely because you believe that in order to 'be a writer' you *must* do so: isn't writing a novel the badge you need in order for others to recognise your bravery in the face of overwhelming odds, like a Victoria Cross, the Legion d'Honneur, or the Medal of Honor?

No. It isn't.

So, if you *are* writing a novel, have you ever stopped to ask yourself if that's the 'best' thing for you to write? The same applies whether you're focussed on a collection of poetry, a play etc. The answer to this fourth question — 'what' — is open to as much challenge as the other three we've already considered.

And you really should challenge it.

Why? Because when we produce our best, most effective, most appropriate work — that which will give us the greatest degree of satisfaction and is likely to make the most of our talents — each of our four answers will be aligned, in harmony.

The 'why', 'who', 'type' and 'what' will be mutually supporting; nothing will be jarring. And it is when we reach this state that the magic happens!

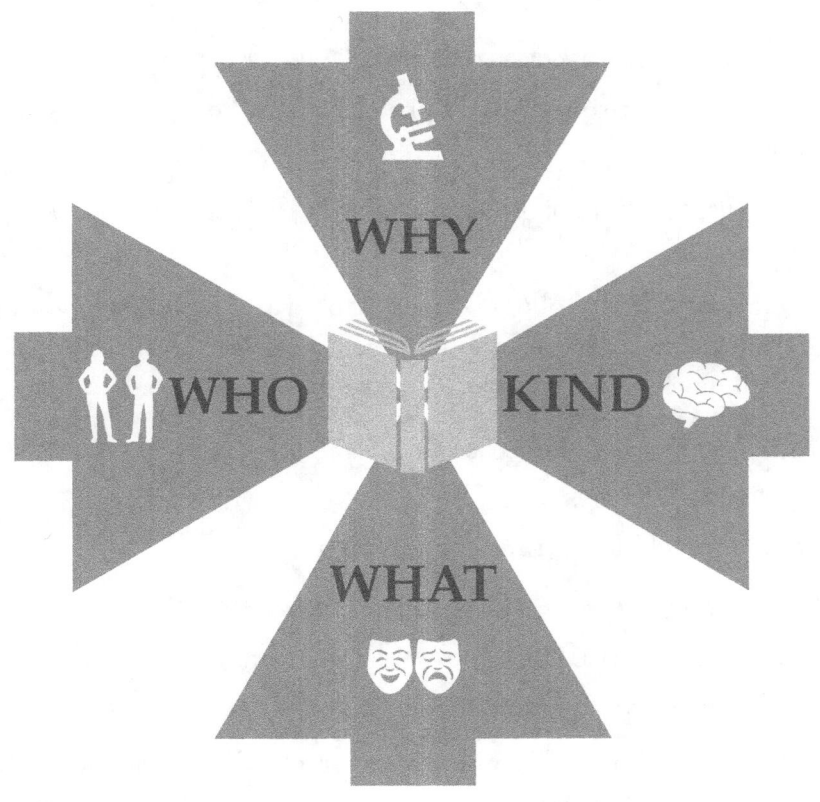

WE HAVE ALREADY SEEN THE DIFFICULTIES AND CONFUSIONS THAT CAN ARISE IF JUST TWO OF THESE ELEMENTS ARE MISALIGNED – AND NOW THERE ARE FOUR!

This is surely justification enough to spend time understanding all four aspects: the why and who of our motivation, our writing approach, and then the 'what' of our projects — the best execution of which can only be built upon cohesion with the rest.

Here are some simple examples of where conflict can arise because you are working on the wrong thing:

'Why?' - you write to make money & 'What?' - you write poetry.

> Well that's a circle that will probably only be squared if you're the poet laureate!

'Type?' - you're a reluctant and occasional writer & 'What?' - you're writing a trilogy of epic novels.

> Okay, so it took Tolkien 17 years to write *Lord of the Rings*, but let's be honest, you're not Tolkien, and so the chances are that you'll never finish what you've started.

'Who?' - you write solely for yourself & 'What?' - you're writing some kind of self-help book for others.

> Ask yourself, is your heart really in it?

'Why?' - you write to be famous and for posterity & 'What?' - an occasional blog without any specific theme, angle, niche, or audience.

> Need I say anything about this one?

There are hundreds of combinations which will be uncomfortable bedfellows, and when this happens you may find yourself struggling.

Most often this struggle manifests itself in difficulty producing the 'what' i.e. the novel's not quite working, the poems are a little 'flat', your genre-worlds are unconvincing etcetera.

REMEMBER, ALL FOUR ELEMENTS OF THIS QUARTET ARE WITHIN YOUR CONTROL AND CAN BE CHANGED TO VARIOUS DEGREES IN ORDER TO IMPROVE YOU AS A WRITER

Why? Be honest about this one; it is the bedrock of everything — yet probably the least flexible of the four. The first step therefore: honest recognition of your writing motivation.

Who? Again this is about recognition and self-awareness. You might not change anything here (e.g. you might not choose to write for someone else) but understanding your primary audience is vital — as in the example where you have a contract/deadline to meet and you need to understand that you aren't really writing for yourself any more.

Type? The process question — and something you *can* change if a) you need to, and b) have the willpower and freedom to do so. The epic fantasy trilogy example above surely demands a structured and robust process rather than a haphazard one! And if you can't change your process — because of the pressures of life or simply because of the way you're made — then recognise and embrace the type of writer you have to be without feeling guilty that you don't conform to some imagined 'ideal' (for example, working 9am-12am or producing 2,000 words a day).

What? Practically the easiest one to change, yet emotionally the most difficult — partly because this is the tangible output, 'where the rubber hits the road'. You may think you should be writing a novel or collection of poetry or a murder mystery, but the previous three answers might not support those as a viable end-product. Look at the 'why', 'who' and 'type', and see if there's an interesting project that *does* fit. If the 'what' is a given — that contract to write a novel! — then you may need to look hard at the other three if the book is not going well. In the examples given two pages earlier, the 'what' simply doesn't fit with the rest of the profile.

Instinctively you will know when these four elements are in synch — indeed, you probably won't need to give them any thought. Your output will demonstrate their alignment.

IN MY 1-2-1 WORK AS A MENTOR I HAVE COME ACROSS PEOPLE WHO WERE STRUGGLING WITH ONE THING – USUALLY THE 'WHAT' – WITHOUT REALISING THE ISSUE WAS ELSEWHERE

Here are real examples from some of my 1-2-1 sessions with writers:

- 'E' who, unable to make any progress on their projects, discovered they were writing not for themselves but for an inner-editor who was continually getting in the way; the 'editor' portion of themselves wanted perfection — and therefore demanded continuous rework. An example of not recognising who they were subconsciously writing for. 'The tyrannical editor' is a very common problem. Given first drafts are never perfect, you need to give yourself permission to write something imperfect and then edit it later, rather than get bogged down and write nothing new at all i.e. the solution is to change the 'who' to one which allows you to be more progressive — and possibly to change the writing process too.

- Having written a successful first novel, 'K' landed a contract for their next book complete with deadline commitments. They were only used to writing for themselves and hadn't got their head around the fact that suddenly writing had become a 'job'. Yes, it was a 'dream job', but now they were writing for someone else, their publisher. Both 'why' and 'who' had changed. They became blocked — to the extent of not even knowing what kind of novel they were supposed to write! — and were hurtling towards a deadline with nothing significant drafted. Recognising the shift in 'why' and 'who' released the breaks and they subsequently managed to hit their first-draft deadline.

- 'S' thought they needed to write a novel — because wasn't that what proved you were a writer? — but were struggling to make progress. On being given an outline of their book, I realised what they had described was actually a connected series of short stories i.e. their perceived 'what' was wrong; they were writing the wrong thing — *and* for the wrong reason. Recognising the short story opportunity freed them, like popping a cork from a bottle! And here is a common warning sign: you justify yourself to other people by uttering the phrase "I'm writing *my* novel…"

- 'P' had successfully finished a non-fiction project and didn't know what to write next. Their main idea was essentially a rehash of what they'd already produced but in a different format. Through discussion we discovered that, whilst there was nothing wrong with the 'concept', they needed to make a conscious change to the 'why' if they still wanted to stay with their original factual theme; they needed to move away from writing for themselves. Not only that, they needed to be more radical in terms of the format of the 'what' they intended to produce. They ended up taking the bones of the non-fiction event and used it as the basis for fiction — which was something they'd always wanted to write anyway!

These are just four examples where misalignment of the basics was preventing the individual concerned from achieving the most they could from their writing.

Do these examples help to validate the approach I'm suggesting? I hope so. Tackling the basic questions — 'why', 'who', 'type', and 'what' — can be a simple exercise undertaken in ten minutes, or mulled over for days. Your choice.

But please don't treat the process superficially, glibly accepting what you think might be 'textbook answers': "I write because I love it"; "I write for myself"; "I write when the muse takes me / when I'm inspired"; "I'm writing my novel". Those answers *may* be right — but I suggest that it's more likely that they are not… or at least not the whole story.

And remember, the final combination(s) you settle on should reflect you, your approach, your beliefs. They should be unique enough to represent the you-as-writer. If you looked at yourself in the mirror as you explained what you were writing (along with the why etcetera) you should recognise and like what you see.

Doing so might also convince the interviewer to offer you that job!

THINGS TO (RE)TRY

Maybe as a teacher would counsel before the beginning of an exam: "take your time — and remember to check your answers!"

And perhaps that's the only recommendation here, an echo of what has already been said. Do the answers 'feel' right? Have you validated them — both individually and together — against your present situation *and* past experiences, both good and bad.

> RECOGNISING WHERE WE HAVE BEEN SUCCESSFUL – OR FAILED – IS WHERE THE REAL GOLD IS HIDDEN

The profile you arrive at should feel like a profile of you as a writer, not you as a person. You may be the nicest person in the world in everyday life, but a tyrant when it comes to your work. Or vice versa!

And remember, **how can you possibly produce your best if you aren't in possession of all the facts** and that ruthless self-knowledge?

So what's next?

Well, what may seem like a few chapters of light relief!

We are going to look at some of the topics already touched on — like being 'a pantser' — in a little more detail; consider some of the weaponry in the writer's arsenal, like editing; challenge "writer's block" and Imposter Syndrome; then look at some technical fundamentals like planning, character profiles, poetry on the page, dialogue and monologue.

Again, the content of these chapters will be based on years of writing experience and on talking with people about writing. They will contain thoughts and suggestions, examples of what might — or might not — work for you. In some places I may be more assertive than others — "this is a good idea; you should do it!" — but in general what follows is a smorgasbord of writerly hints and tips.

But how does all this relate to what we've already covered? Well, if the 'why', 'who', 'type' and 'what' are the bricks of our writing edifice, the rest contribute to the render, elements of decoration, the style of the windows etcetera all of which go up to make the final construct.

And at the end?

Hopefully you'll be in a better place to write — not only psychologically, but practically too. And maybe you'll have answered the original question in a way that is both positive and satisfying..!

"TELL ME WHAT THE ANSWER IS…"

One of the things which constantly surprises me is how many people believe there are 'right answers' to writing-related conundrums. "How should I…", "How do you…", "What's the right way to…"

Such questions arise at writing retreats and courses, in response to prompts and exercises, or during casual conversations. More often than you might imagine, I have known people to be striving to find the 'silver bullet' which will help them move their work forward, resolve an issue with which they are struggling, or make their work brilliant and them successful.

If it does anything, I would like to think that attempting to answer the 'why', 'who', 'type' and 'what' questions demonstrates that there are no 'right answers'.

Think about it; if there were right answers would James Joyce have written *Ulysses* or Ezra Pound *The Cantos*?

THERE ARE NO RIGHT ANSWERS – THOUGH THERE MAY BE A PLETHORA OF WRONG ONES

How can that make sense?

Where there are right answers they will tend to manifest themselves in general terms rather than specifics: you shouldn't steal, copy or plagiarise; you should always be honest with yourself; you should write about what you want to write about, not what you think you should be writing about (though the latter is often associated with "how can I make the most money?" or "how can I be read?"); you should always dedicate yourself to editing, and not treat it as a necessary evil or something to be avoided; you should seek opinions and, if asked to do so, you should critique kindly — because one day it will be you on the receiving end...

And you should never stop writing.

WRITING IS A NEVER-ENDING APPRENTICESHIP - AND LIKE ALL APPRENTICESHIPS, THE MORE YOU PRACTICE THE LESS YOU NEED SOMEONE TO TEACH YOU

THINGS TO TRY

Even if you concede that there are few 'right' answers, it is natural to occasionally find yourself wanting to land on something concrete in relation to writing, especially if you find you can articulate your question in specific terms.

Perhaps you want to find a reliable way of doing X or Y. If so, perhaps try this approach:

- Write down the question you want answered, and do so in as much detail as possible: "I want to know X, perhaps because of A and B."

- Then try and break the question down, either by expanding what X means or by analysing A and B. For example:

  <u>"I want to know how many words I should write in a day."</u>
  - Why? "Because I find about 500 is my limit."
  - Why? "Because with work and the family I don't have that much time to write."
  - Answer: If you want to write more you need to *make* the time, which may be possible if you can sacrifice something else (the week's third trip to the gym, perhaps). Alternatively, you will need accept the constraints life

imposes on you and recognise that 500 is the 'right' target word count for you — at least at the present time. So don't beat yourself up over it.

...or...

"Tell me how to write free verse."

- Why? "Because all my poetry rhymes, and I only seem to be able to write sonnets."

- So why change? "Because proper poets write free verse."

- Who says? Perhaps you aren't 'wired' to write free verse — in the same way that an even larger proportion of poets can't write sonnets.

- Answer: Ask yourself different questions — perhaps the ones you should be asking. Firstly, are you maximising the quality of what you are producing? I would challenge you to assert that your sonnets are the best you can make them. If not, why not? In any event, to write other things you need to experiment and explore — and to be prepared to fail. So second question: how often have you tried to write free verse? Or read free verse come to that! If you're truly serious about a different style or genre, you have to put in the hard yards, the effort, the grind — which could take years, and many failures. Is one of your underlying issues that you find failure difficult and therefore shy away from the trying? You see how the questions shift when examined? Alternatively (or additionally) you could try a course on the assumption that nothing beats an intensive period of focus when you're trying to learn something new.

These may be slightly fanciful examples I agree, but the point is that in seeking a 'silver bullet' you may be trying to answer the *wrong* question e.g. the dilemma about 500 words might not have been about volume at all, but rather the environment in which those words were produced.

The only other thing to suggest at this point is to try and elucidate those things that are truly bothering you — and then to formulate them as questions. Doing so can give you something to work with.

One aid in this area might be to keep a notebook where you log your thoughts about your writing. Make no mistake, this is not a diary nor somewhere you write creatively, but rather a place where you can unpack all those questions and uncertainties. You may find that in forcing yourself to make them concrete, putting pen to paper and then later revisiting what you have written, solutions may become apparent. I have kept a series of such notebooks for forty years and in them I can trace ideas, concerns, even progress towards resolution[2]. Within their pages there are, for example, ideas for the plots of novels, multiple notions as to how I might maximise my writing time / output, fancy schemes relating to hours per day or words per day, and so forth. I was trying to answer a specific question and having the related debate with myself certainly helped. But in the end what *actually* worked was trying various things out until I settled on the ones that best suited me i.e. that helped align 'why', 'who', 'type' and 'what'.

Most questions you may have *can* be answered, but not in a simple or rudimentary way — and often only by working hard, through trial and error.

"SHOW UP. DIG DEEP. DO THE WORK." – KERRI MAHER

---

[2] A compilation of these notebook entires can be found in *Shrapnel from a Writing Life*, Coverstory books, 2020

PERSONA / BRAND: DOES IT MATTER?

Imagine you're in a supermarket buying tomato ketchup or mayonnaise or frozen food. All other things being equal — including the price — do you choose the well-known quality branded item or the somewhat anonymous-looking own brand? Or you're flying across the Atlantic and have the option between really good seats on a world-leading airline or cheap seats on a budget flyer, who would be your carrier of choice?

We live in an age which is dominated by advertising and branding. Watch just about any television programme on just about any channel and it will be interrupted by adverts, all trying to persuade us to buy a product or to elevate one above another. I wonder how much has been spent in the Coca Cola™ versus Pepsi™ image wars over the years...

Whether it's 'in-your-face' advertising or something more subtle like product placement, we are bombarded with promotional material all the time. Some of it is super-subtle. Did you know that many stores and High Street institutions even have their own perfume, a scent that is pumped around each and every one of their locations as a means of reinforcing brand, of confirming to you that — by smell alone! — you know whose shop you are in?

Why should writers be any different — though not in the realm of scent, obviously!

If your aim is to stand out in any way from the millions of other writers — and not just those in your immediate circle — how are you going to do that? Because the truth is that your writing alone isn't going to do it for you.

Many of us hope our work will be good enough, exceptional enough, to lift us above our peers and allow us to been seen as 'first among equals'. But will it? Is it realistic to think that, in a contemporary world with a plethora of ways to expose all sorts of creative work into an already overwhelmed readership, what we write will be sufficient to do all that heavy lifting?

Of course not.

Which begs a question — and returns us to our original 'why do you write?' and 'who do you write for?' conundrums:

DO YOU <u>REALLY</u> WANT TO BE A WRITER WHO STANDS OUT FROM THE CROWD?

Over the coming chapters we will find, time and again, that in examining various aspects of writing we can reference back to those original three questions — 'why', 'who', and 'type' — and in doing so both reinforce their importance *and* demonstrate that how we answer them can influence other tangential aspects of writing. Like persona and brand.

And I say again, **the quality of your writing has absolutely nothing to do with *guaranteeing* success.**

But also consider this: in the same way great writing doesn't ensure public recognition, neither does 'bad' writing disqualify it.

Sounds illogical, unreasonable? Of course it does — but it's true. We may know really good writers who are invisible to the rest of the world; and we can probably all point to 'popular' writers who — we might argue — don't write at all well. Even global sensations. If that is indeed the case, then how have they 'made it'? Answer: luck plays a huge part — but it may also be that they didn't only sell their writing, they sold themselves too.

Take a look on Instagram or TikTok and you will find people who — irrespective of the quality of their work — claim to be writers and have vast legions of followers. Like it or not, they are selling something that is appealing to a certain kind of readership, and are delivering it through a medium which suits that audience.

And medium is vitally important. Forty years ago there was only one: the printed word. If you wanted to get noticed, be read, you had to find yourself an agent and a publisher; you had to get your words into bookshops. Back then the quality of what you produced was of far greater importance than it is now. We live in a world of technological democratisation. If you have a computer, a webcam, a microphone, you can expose your work on any number of platforms — and can have an ebook available for sale on Amazon in the blink of an eye.

Yet that guarantees nothing.

In the relentless commoditisation of the twenty-first century, merely having a presence — perhaps one personal website — isn't enough. This is partly because there are millions of people continually shouting into the void and trying to be heard in the cacophony — and also because there is so little *difference* between those voices. Browse through Instagram and you will see dozens — if not hundreds or thousands — of young women all trying to be 'seen', recognised, acknowledged. Their approach is to follow what has become *the* contemporary and superficial formula for 'beauty'. The consequence is that <u>none</u> of them are particularly distinguishable from each another; their individuality is lost in a homogenous mass.

Such a reality prompts the questions that you, as a writer, must ask yourself: not only 'why do you write?', but those on the layer beneath that, including:

ARE YOU PREPARED TO DO WHAT IT TAKES TO BE RECOGNISED AS 'DIFFERENT'?

And if the answer to that question is 'yes', then the follow-on question is the slightly disbelieving echo 'really and truly?'...

Because to get there, to be recognised, **has almost nothing to do with your writing**.

IT'S ALL ABOUT YOU; NOT WHO YOU ARE, BUT HOW YOU WISH TO BE SEEN

'Brand' is the term usually applied to an endeavour to be identified and differentiated. Think Coca Cola™ and Pepsi™. We're talking about you as 'product'. But if it's helpful — and given that you're a person — then 'persona' might be equally appropriate. Unless you are made in a particular way, it might be that you need to create a second persona: your writer's persona. These days there are experienced marketeers who specialise in helping writers promote themselves, just as there are many individuals and organisations who can help you build 'a presence'.

Suddenly there's you the everyday individual, the person you have always been, and then this new, public-facing version of yourself.

Is that what you want?

THE QUESTIONS YOU NEED TO ASK YOURSELF...

The fundamental question is the one above about being recognised as 'different' — which also harks back to where we started this book: 'why do you write?' and what do you want from your writing?

And once you have answered, once you have confirmed that you *do* want to be seen, recognised etcetera, there are a number of follow-on questions:

Is your personality suited to being more outgoing, visible - even virtually? Do you have the self-confidence to carry it off?

In a sense this is about authenticity. Even if your 'writer persona' is in part fabrication, it still needs to come across as the genuine you. If you create a persona you do not believe in even while inhabiting it, then how can it not come across to others as shallow, clichéd, a caricature?

It is also about your natural demeanour. If you are inherently shy or introverted, creating this 'second you' will be difficult though not impossible. And remember, this new persona needs to be assertive; it needs to represent a version of yourself which *believes* you have a right to be centre stage, to he heard, to be listened to. You need to believe that you *are* different.

Do you think that your writing is 'good enough'? (because it really should be!)

Part of that difference, your right to trumpet yourself and your work, *has* to be that you honestly believe your writing is good enough to stand up to the additional scrutiny you will be inviting. You may have successfully created a positive personal impression, but if your new readers find your work is substandard... Well, there's no way back.

'Imposter syndrome' — the bane of many a writer's life — can be a challenge too. But if you do suffer from it, that doesn't necessarily disqualify you from wanting to create a brand, a second persona. It's just another factor which makes doing so harder.

What makes you 'different'? (i.e. you're not just 'some other writer' akin to all those young women on Instagram)

> What are you selling — not yourself this time, but your work? If there is nothing fresh, original, unique or distinctive about it you may struggle. Quality can help, of course: okay, you write run-of-the-mill sci-fi, but you write it really, really well. Tick.
>
> Your difference might be described in terms of voice or style or the way you weave your plots — but you need to be able to articulate it if challenged, and to defend it. Indeed, if you are going to 'have a presence' — a website or some other social media vehicle — that difference will need to be evident there too, because that's where the majority of your new readers will encounter you for the first time.

Do you have the time (and possibly money) to put in to your reinvention?

> There is work involved. If you are going to set-up a website, a blog, a YouTube channel or a Substack site, in the early days as you establish your 'channels' (you see, marketing-speak!) these things will take a lot of effort. This is a new demand which can only be met by finding more time or by doing it in place of something else, like writing… There is a balance to be struck. In some cases — as with a Substack or Wordpress site, for example — you may be able to find a way to harmonise both writing and brand creation, but balance will be key. So consider the demands on your time.

Do you have the necessary skills?

> Many of the opportunities open to you in terms of brand or persona creation will involve technology: the use of the internet, the ability to manipulate site-building toolsets. Certainly you can learn those skills, but it may take a while if you are a complete novice — and some people simply don't function in a way that is 'technology compatible'. Is that you?

Amazon KDP, which allows you to create an ebook and sell it (exclusively) on their Kindle store, requires some fairly sophisticated manipulation of their platform to create a good end product. If you don't understand what you are doing then your book will betray your inexperience and blow a hole in your credibility. Take a look at the covers of some self-published Kindle novels; many are obviously amateurish. Why would a reader part with their money for those? Remember, your persona needs to be authentic — but it also needs to be *credible*.

Can you articulate why you want to 'be seen' in such a way as to really believe in the project (for that's what it will become) — and can you describe the end goal, what the future will look like if you are successful?

Forgive me for going back to the beginning, but this really is the crux of the matter. The 'why'. *Why* are you going to spend all this time and energy? *Why* are you going to put in the extra effort? In short, what's in it for you? Because surely there must be something, an end goal. Yours is a project which may be designed to change your life in some way — so recognise it as such. Not only that, but you should articulate *how* your life will be different. If the creation of your brand / writer persona actually works and gets you noticed, if your writing is good enough to support it, *and* if it delivers those things you hope for, what does your future look like? How will next Monday be different to last Monday? Make the change concrete in your mind; manifest it; fill it with specifically imagined things.

If, for example, you get to the end of this self-examination and declare that your new brand / persona will enable you to become famous or rich, then revisit your original reason for being a writer. I would be prepared to bet that being rich and famous never figured! And, to be frank, it's almost certain that you'll never get there.

UNDERTAKING A BRAND / PERSONA CREATION PROJECT CAN REALLY EXPOSE WHY YOU ARE WRITING AND WHO YOU WANT TO BE AS A WRITER

It can also prove that, in reality, you want none of the faff; you simply want a quiet life, and to be left alone to write.

And that's okay!

...AND THINGS TO TRY

Not only should you try to answer all the questions above — and revisit the first one with which we started this journey — but you could also:

- Pick someone you know and admire, and see if you can establish the profile of their writing life — then ask yourself if that's what you really want, up at 4 a.m. and writing 5 or 6 hours per day...

- Invest time in searching the internet to find those people or companies who might help you on your 'brand journey' — then ask yourself if you want to spend your money to get their assistance.

- Also trawl the usual suspects in terms of 'channels' (i.e. Facebook, Twitter/X, Instagram etcetera) and see how those are being used by 'visible' writers: what they are posting, how often they are posting and so forth. Which of those mediums appeal most to you, and do you think you can establish and then maintain the kind of drumbeat they require?

- Enter competitions. Getting a few good results under your belt can help establish you as a 'serious writer' and give you credibility both locally and in the wider writing community. At the extreme end of the spectrum, I wonder how many more copies of a book are sold if the cover is emblazoned with "Pulitzer Prize winner"...

- Try and find an agent — though be prepared for *many* rejections. However, if you fail to land an agent and win nothing in competitions this activity can act as a sobering sense-check on your ambitions.

If you find all of the above daunting then, to be honest, I'm glad. <u>It is daunting</u>. And if you think I'm trying to put you off making the leap then guilty as charged, partly because it's really hard to be successful. You're trying to be identified as an individual branch in a forest of trees — which I suppose is a step up from being merely a leaf in a forest of trees! (Which, by the way, is probably where most writers are happiest...)

But there's another, more serious serious point.

BEING A 'BRAND' OR HAVING A 'WRITER PERSONA' MAY SIMPLY NOT BE YOU

You may well invest huge amounts of time and energy — and money, who knows? — and in the end, successful or not, be profoundly unhappy; you could find yourself tied to a life you hate, or have to face up to not making any progress at all and in consequence feel an unmitigated failure.

Doesn't all of this demonstrate the supreme value in asking yourself the 'why do you write?' question? Do you need to ask yourself that question again — right now?

Oh, but before you give up on the whole shebang, one final thing: you may not need to have a 'brand' in order to be 'a writer'... It's not for everyone.

THE CHALLENGE OF ORIGINALITY

If you are a writer of fiction then you may have come across this theory: **There are only seven plots -** Overcoming the monster; Rags to riches; The quest; Voyage and return; Comedy; Tragedy; Rebirth.[3]

Well, that's that then.

But wait. Booker identifies two other plots — Mystery, and Rebellion against 'The One' — though he dislikes these apparently because "they are less about the main character embracing his feminine side." (Glen Strathy, how-to-write-a-book-now.com)

So maybe it isn't as simple as there being only seven plots; after all Booker's assertion is based on decades of analysis from a particular Jungian viewpoint. Presumably if you took another tack you might come up with a different answer...

And what about sub-plot types, because there are those too?

As a species we tend to the reductive, we embrace simplicity, like to label things, put them in boxes; and yes, most scholars agree with the seven plot list. The theory is that you can fit every story into one of these, and in some cases — *The Odyssey*, for example — probably into more than one.

SO WHAT?

What possible benefit accrues from you being able to tag your narrative in such a way? Indeed, I would argue it would be more instructive if you could not!

---

[3] *The Seven Basic Plots*, Christopher Booker, 2004

The problem with a list such as Brooker's is that it may suggest there is a something you *should* be writing, and that if you can align your story with one of the seven then you're 'ok'. But as we've already discovered, defining things in writing is never that simple.

For example, I typed 'narrative style' into Google and was informed that there were four: linear, non-linear, descriptive, and viewpoint (indeed.com, essaypro.com). But then elsewhere I was informed that there were an alternative four: first person, third person outside, third person inside, and omniscient — with second person (*clearly* a valid narrative style) being roundly dismissed! (thewritersguide.co.uk)

So no agreement as to what 'narrative style' means then…

And you don't have to look too far to find generalisations such as this: "Everything already exists. The ideas, plots, characters, language, and subject matter — they're already out there in someone else's work." (writingforward.com)

Depressing? No, not depressing; **irrelevant**.

ORIGINALITY ISN'T ARRIVED AT THROUGH SUBJECT MATTER, BUT WITH VOICE

Here's an example.

When the world was hit with the Covid-19 pandemic in 2020 writers were presented with a brand new *specific* subject that had never been written about before. How could it have been? Suddenly tens of thousands of people were writing about Covid: poems, short stories, plays, novels. In consequence there was a great deal of 'bad writing' — as there has been recently about the wars in Ukraine and Gaza — and almost in an instant the subject matter became hackneyed, a cliché. Here was a demonstration how quality work and originality came not from any uniqueness in the overall 'plot' or 'theme' per se, but in how it was treated.

Consider these:

"Originality isn't coming up with something new; it's using your imagination to put old concepts together in new ways." (writingforward.com)

"Originality in writing means integrating your own authentic voice into what you are trying to say. We all have authentic voices, and integrating that voice into your writing is important. An original voice does not mean you have to write about a new idea, although you might. Rather, it means making it your own." (pressbooks.library.torontomu.ca)

If you wanted to, I'm sure you could harvest dozens of similar quotes.

ORIGINALITY RESIDES IN HOW YOU TELL THE STORY

Would you not agree that the film/musical *West Side Story* is original? Yet the plot is a rehash of *Romeo and Juliet*. And indeed many of Shakespeare's own plots were stolen from others' earlier work. The originality was in the writing, the words chosen, how one followed on from another.

It's impossible to know how many love poems have ever been written. Millions without doubt. And the ones we remember? Nothing to do with the subject, but rather the talent of the writer, the perspective they offer on the subject.

And the ones we forget? Badly written, bland, clichéd, lacking uniqueness.

"TELL ALL THE TRUTH BUT TELL IT SLANT" - EMILY DICKINSON

The problem with 'originality' — or the *perceived* problem with originality — has nothing to do with what you are writing about. For example, you don't need to try and invent some fantastical new and unique world for your sci-fi narrative to make it a great story — Orwell's *1984* is not a million miles away from contemporary life.

Or think about murder mysteries, especially those dramatised for TV. Isn't there always a scene with the police team having a discussion around a whiteboard of some kind, usually laden with photographs? Or an apparent 'bad guy' who turns out not to be so? Can you not predict what comes next, or tick off the standard scenes as if you were playing 'murder mystery bingo'? Yet sometimes this repetition doesn't matter — and when it doesn't matter that's because it has been written very well, or perhaps slightly 'slant'.

ALL OF WHICH PUTS A DIFFERENT 'ORIGINALITY' PRESSURE ON THE WRITER

For poets and the writers of plays and screenplays the challenge of originality has a different complexion compared to the author of fiction — and not only in that the 'seven plots' theory may not apply in the same way.

Playwrights have additional tools at their disposal when it comes to asserting originality; they are not entirely bound by the page. Partly this is because their words are spoken, but also because they have 'space' to play with: the dimensions of the stage and how that is furnished. Think about *King Lear*. The same words, more or less the same physical confines of the stage, yet no two productions have *ever* been identical.

And for screenwriters: the frame of a screen, the myriad of potential locations, the infinite possibilities of CGI. And in both mediums, sound can be overlaid too.

Unless you go back to poetry's spoken origins, traditionally a poet has been bound by words and the page — which is one of the reasons why many seek 'originality' (or 'difference') in terms of how their words are laid out: printed landscape, weird justifications, blocks of redaction or blackness, bizarre fonts and formatting. The use of 'white space' has become a valid stylistic device. Recently — and even more ridiculously! — some writers have started using emojis and not words at all…

You can see how use of such 'techniques' quickly catapults a poem into gimmickry; and there is a consequent danger of readers assuming that because a poem 'looks different' it is therefore 'original' and therefore 'good' — when in fact much of that gimmickry is merely a veneer to cover-up sub-standard writing. Perhaps more than in any other written form, poetry stands or falls on the very few *words* used.

It is not surprising to see the recent rise in performance poetry. Reading their own work allows a poet control over the delivery of their words i.e. they do not need to rely on whacky page formatting to be the attention-grabber; the distinctiveness comes from both the words *and* the poet making themselves the medium, the transport between poem and 'reader'.

THE QUESTIONS YOU NEED TO ASK YOURSELF…

Originality is, therefore, both easy to aspire to and yet difficult to attain — especially if one also aims to write something of quality. Often pursuit of originality can lead a writer into the use of gimmicks, the result of asking themselves the wrong questions or misunderstanding what 'originality' actually is. Inadvertently they can adopt what they perceive to be original but which, by the time they have employed it, has become clichéd. I knew someone who was writing a thriller loosely based on their professional life experience. Their fiction was not only over-written, but it was filled with scenes unconsciously stolen from cinema. When I read it, all too often I thought "yes, I've seen that film"... They were trying desperately to be original, yet were producing something that was almost the complete opposite.

So how do we know when we're being original? None of us sets out to produce imitation or pastiche, and surely being the individual doing the writing — we are using *our* words, after all! — how can what we come up with be anything other than original?

But remember, 'originality' is established less via narrative than through style or voice.

"USING YOUR IMAGINATION TO PUT OLD CONCEPTS TOGETHER IN NEW WAYS" & **"ORIGINALITY IN WRITING MEANS INTEGRATING YOUR OWN AUTHENTIC VOICE INTO WHAT YOU ARE TRYING TO SAY"**

So rather than being associated with totally *new* subject matter, originality primarily comes down to 'voice'.

How can we possibly know if we have an 'original voice'? Indeed, whether we have a unique voice at all?

> There will be very few people — *very few people* — who find their 'voice' right off the bat. When we start writing we're usually imitating (unconsciously or otherwise) what we like to read in terms of fiction or poetry, or see in the case of screenplays/plays. How can we not do otherwise? It can take a great deal of practice — and lots of writing! — in order to find a style of writing which feels natural and comfortable. Years, in fact.

How can you tell if you've found your voice? Most likely when others recognise it: "When I read this poem I could hear you reading it". Or, when you try and write in a different style, you find yourself gravitating back to the one where you're most at home — and this can include subject matter as well as how you put one word after another. Try writing Romance when you're really at home in the world of Thrillers; well, you're unlikely to be either happy or convincing.

And an original voice? I'm not really sure that there are many truly original voices any more. Remember that comment about everything having already been written? I think that may apply to styles too, and if that is the case much of any 'newness' left is either a subtle twist on what has already been established and written, or merely the gimmicky.

My argument, therefore, isn't that you should try and be different; rather, that you should try and be *authentic* and produce the best writing you possibly can. If you are lucky enough to be able to marry quality with a 'voice', a style, a way of looking at things 'slant', and of "integrating that voice into your writing", then you've half a chance.

What can we do in order to refine our voice?

The answer is rather dull. First, just write — and don't stop. And second, when writing, try other styles, other voices (e.g. like the Romance vs. Thriller example above). Find the things that <u>don't</u> work for you, then ruthlessly abandon them. First-person, second-person, third-person, past or present, stream-of-consciousness; try them all. Or try writing prose like Austen or poetry like Auden; seek out difficulty and complexity, recognise pastiche and cheap imitation — then eliminate the latter from your work. Eventually you will find that you start coming back to a theme, a style that fits you.

But be ready for the gut-punch: you might indeed find that combination, that voice, the one which fits you like a glove — and then not like it. What if you naturally write like Dickens, but really want to craft stories like Dan Brown? That's really hard to face. Your choices will probably boil down to being the best Dickens-like writer you can be, or to keep imitating Dan Brown knowing you are unlikely to ever succeed.

How do you tell if what we have written has anything unique about it?

At the simplest level ask yourself whether your work stands out in a crowd as being clearly 'yours'. Writing groups — if a safe environment and run in such a way so as to give honest and constructive feedback — can be useful as a guide.

In any event, you can stand back from what you have written and ask yourself — honestly, mind! — whether anyone else could have produced the same piece of work, both subject and voice. And if your answer is 'no' (which will be the instinctive response of course!) then challenge yourself to identify what it is that makes the work undeniably yours. I have been in writing groups where you *know* that really funny poem could only have been written by X, the pathos-filled prose by Y.

Honesty is particularly critical here. Remember the comment earlier in the book about work with Covid-19 as the subject? Most of the pieces I read at the time could have been written by anyone; they were generic, homogenous, amorphous. The best ones came at the topic from a unique angle, with a 'slant', an approach that didn't overtly claim "here is *the* definitive Covid poem". And you can apply that same judgement to fiction too. Perhaps the most extreme example will be 'Mills & Boon' romances. Because they are so formulaic, almost any member of their stable of authors could have written any of the stories in their genre: 'Doctors & Nurses'; 'Rich Man, Poor Girl' etcetera. If that's what you want to write, fine; but I would argue there's nothing truly unique about it — even though *you* may have written it. The 'voice' is a 'Mills & Boon' voice, not yours.

How can you manipulate form in order to better suit your style, your voice, and the message you're trying to convey?

In some respects it's easier for those writing plays or scripts to experiment in this area. During rehearsals or early takes they can try out sound effects, movement, positioning actors in different locations, all with the aim of making what they are attempting to say more effective, to change the environment in which their words are delivered. Film-makers too have the ability to manipulate those things which wrap around their words during editing; the ability to adjust timing is perhaps their greatest tool. [You can adjust timing in poetry and prose too. Perhaps think about how you might do so. Experiment.]

For those denied such ornamentation, the only 'form' available for manipulation is in the choice of words and how those words look on the page (physical or virtual). As has already been pointed out, the dividing line between meaningful and considered creative enhancement and shallow gimmickry is a very narrow one — and I suspect there is more real estate on the gimmicky side!

Fiction writers can play with chapter lengths, line justification, paragraph size and so forth. Increasingly you see novels with varying fonts or non-linguistic elements inserted. If you are tempted to do so, by all means have a play — but be prepared to answer the question as to *why* you have set your text out in the way you have. And be prepared for it not to work — as in the unreadable two-column layout of DBC Pierre's *Meanwhile in Dopamine City* (my opinion, obviously). Mere 'difference' is not an adequate reason to let something stand.

Poets have even more freedom: not only in stanza choice and their sizes (or no stanzas at all), but line lengths, the number of words on a line, or words on a page, the amount of white space etcetera. Word processing software makes trying some of these things out easy too. Take a draft poem and rather than have the lines left-justified, centre them; it can make a piece feel radically different, transformative even — and all for a couple of seconds' effort. If you *have* to, test out the wacky stuff, but in such cases not only be ready to justify your reason for doing so, but be wary of the form becoming the poem i.e. where the words are relegated to the irrelevant partner and you find that you've ended up with something that isn't really a poem at all.

Sadly there is more and more of such nonsense about, and even the Forward Prize has succumbed to praise some of it.

SO, TRY. BE PREPARED TO FAIL. AND REMEMBER,
'DIFFERENCE' DOESN'T EQUAL ORIGINALITY OR QUALITY

INSPIRATION — OR 'THE MUSE'

Where do ideas come from? That's a valid question. Indeed, it's one I have been asked myself. The answer? Perhaps everywhere, and nowhere — which is, of course, code for 'there is no right answer'. Or 'we're all different'. Or 'it depends…'

"But surely" (I hear you claim) "there can't be *that* many sources of inspiration." Well, if you want to be reductive, let's go down that route:

THERE ARE ONLY TWO SOURCES OF INSPIRATION: INTERNAL AND EXTERNAL

How's that?

Okay, it's simplistic, but hardly illuminating or helpful. If 'external' are those things that influence us from outside our individual selves and which act upon us, then 'internal' represent the ideas and notions generated by our own thoughts.

Still not enough. We need to go further, to sub-divide. Shall we say 'Internal, passive' and 'Internal, active'? And I'm partly indebted to George Saunders for thinking about splitting the notion this way.[4]

Internal, passive

These are ideas which come to us unbidden; that unexpected moment — in the middle of the night, in the shower, over dinner, on a bus etc. — when we 'suddenly think of something'. And these ideas are generally <u>unrelated</u> to what we were doing at the time e.g. in the shower, on the bus etc.

---

[4] cf. "Thinking about a work in progress" on George Saunders' Substack, *Story Club*

'A FLASH OF INSPIRATION' – OR A VISITATION FROM 'THE MUSE'

We have absolutely no control over such moments. They cannot be conjured up. They obey no laws, no patterns, no logical sequence of events.

For many people, 'internal passive' ideas are sacrosanct, nirvana, proof that the Muse exists — and that they are truly blessed having such insight. Those who rely on the internal passive to kick-start their writing cannot, therefore, operate in a methodical way; it is not uncommon for such people to be 'go with the flow' writers who wait for inspiration to strike. Their output may be sporadic as a result.

Internal, active

We sit down at our desk with a problem that needs to be solved: what happens next in this story? How do I navigate successfully between these two scenes? Should this poem rhyme or not? And so forth. These are examples of the 'internal active' idea i.e. when we purposefully try and come up with something. While this activity often has a specific focus (as in the rudimentary examples above), it could also be far more general: "what shall I write next?"

If you wanted to be a little more expansive, you might say that we are being *active* when we go searching for idea, whereas we are being *passive* when ideas seek us out.

And what about 'external' sources then? Surely there are similarities. Shall we subdivide those too?

External, passive

Again we are in one of those moments when we are not looking for inspiration. We are likely to be occupied in some other activity — indeed, anything other than writing. But then something happens <u>related</u> to the activity in which we are engaged or in our environment which strikes us as subject matter we could use creatively.

Let's take riding a bus as an example If you were going along looking out of the window and had a sudden thought about a piece you were working on or had a notion to write a story about an astronaut in space, those are *internal passive* ideas. But if you saw something happen through the window or on the bus itself and that action immediately struck you as a thing to be interpreted and written about, then that is an *external passive* idea i.e. the active ingredient was 'outside' of yourself and was also not something for which you were looking.

External, active

As with internal active, external active is also you probing for an idea — but in this instance you are deliberately placing yourself in a situation where you are hoping the outside world will feed you material.

The best example I can think of is the café. You go to a café, order a coffee, place yourself in a location which gives you a good view of the clientele, then you open your notebook and scan for an idea. You might 'steal' the couple from the next table and invent a history for them, or the businessman who has just walked in looking stressed and hastily orders a takeout; you might overhear a nearby conversation and decide to use that as the bones of something. In essence, you have put yourself in a situation where you are saying "Okay world, here I am and I'm ready; feed me!"

~

It is entirely possible that, of the four scenarios outlined above, you will have a preferred approach to harvesting ideas: you either 'go looking' or 'wait for the Muse', and do so publicly or in the privacy of your home. And that's fine. Whatever suits you as a writer. But whichever way you are naturally inclined, the truth is that we have no control over any of the four:

- Internal passive: you can have no knowledge as to when inspiration will strike; there could be months between good ideas — and then a bunch might come all in a rush.
- Internal active: sitting down to 'study' and expecting to find an idea — and a good one at that — guarantees nothing; you could spend hours staring at a blank page or only surface the really dreadful.
- External passive: given the source of this inspiration is external, not only can you not control your environment, you can never know when — or if — an idea might arrive. Luck plays a huge part: right place, right time…
- External active: yes, you are being proactive in such situations, but you are still at the mercy of chance. What if all the patrons in the café are 'boring'? What if there are no interesting conversations to be overheard?

No right answers, remember?

RELYING ON ONE SOLE SOURCE OF INSPIRATION FOR YOUR IDEAS IS SIMPLY NONSENSICAL

The good news for us is that these four channels are not mutually exclusive. Far from it. They are always present, always available. We cannot 'turn off' the passive channels — even when we're asleep! — and it is only with the active ones that we have choice i.e. choosing to put ourselves in situations where we might 'find' something to inspire us: at our desk, or in a café, a park, the shopping mall.

And why is all this relevant? Firstly because it is useful to recognise where ideas come from; secondly, because it might encourage you to expand how you actively search for ideas and be less reliant on 'magic happening'; and thirdly, because it ties back to to one of our primary questions i.e. what 'type' of writer you are.

THE QUESTIONS YOU NEED TO ASK YOURSELF...

Even though this section of the book is more about informing and suggesting rather than explicit questioning, there are still some things for you to consider.

Does what you regard as your primary source of inspiration fit with how you see yourself as a writer?

> We've already hinted at this. Consider the incompatible combinations: you claim to be a structured and methodical writer, yet get all of your ideas in an internal passive way; or you like to 'go with the flow' yet insist on trying to force ideas through 'active' means.
>
> If such an incompatibility applies to you then it could be that either your assessment of the type of writer you are is incorrect, or you are not adequately exploring the most appropriate sources of inspiration.

Do you invest sufficient time and effort in the two proactive channels?

> Make no mistake, actively seeking ideas requires effort, time, and discipline: you need to force yourself to sit at your desk and stare at a notebook or keyboard; you have to make the effort to go to the café in order to observe people. It can be all too easy — and too tempting! — to just wait for the ideas 'to come'.

That's not to say such an approach is 'wrong' in any way; it may suit you, your style, your personality. But you may be missing out on opportunities and as a result not writing as much as you want to. And why? Because you're not getting the ideas...

Which source of inspiration best suits what you are writing — because yes, there is an alignment to the 'what' of your writing too!

Let's say that you have decided to write a collection of short stories, each of them based on the imagined lives of a number of individuals and touching on certain 'themes' in those lives: birth, death, relationships etcetera. If you are simply sitting at home waiting for those fictional characters to magically appear before you, then you could be waiting a long time. Not only that, but they may end up being remarkably similar.

But if you were to go where people were — or at least the 'essence' of people — then you would have access to a much greater variety of source material. Not only somewhere like a café, but on a bus or train, in a museum or gallery, or even walking through a graveyard and creating your individuals based on the names from old gravestones.

...AND THINGS TO TRY

Obviously consider the questions above, and — as with so many of the threads within this book — take the time to triangulate one answer with another. Remember, so much about being a 'successful' writer depends on you knowing yourself as thoroughly as possible.

THE MYTH THAT IS "WRITER'S BLOCK"

Here is my opening gambit:

THERE IS NO SUCH THING AS "WRITER'S BLOCK"

But having made such a statement, I am beholden to try and understand the nature of the so-named affliction from which many writers claim to suffer — and to consider whether there are any circumstances under which they may use "writer's block" to abdicate responsibility for a lack of productivity…

Let's start with a definition:

- "Writer's block is a non-medical condition, primarily associated with writing, in which an author is either unable to produce new work or experiences a creative slowdown… Writer's block has various degrees of severity, from difficulty in coming up with original ideas to being unable to produce work for years… The majority of writer's block researchers agree that most causes of writer's block have an affective/physiological, motivational, and cognitive component." - Wikipedia

Given this definition is punctuated with symptoms, it reads a little like a medical diagnosis. Perhaps the best way to attack the complaint, therefore, is to go after those symptoms.

And for clarity, accepting that "writer's block" is 'a non-medical condition', any strict physical or mental impediment to writing such as illness or incapacity — essentially the physiological and cognitive — is completely beyond the scope of this brief analysis.

Let's dive in…

"unable to produce new work" / "difficulty in coming up with original ideas"

How do you define 'unable' — and what do you mean by 'new work' or 'original ideas'?

Let's take the second part first: 'new work' & 'original ideas'. Is this an inability to drum up inspiration, new things to write about, or a more broad complaint i.e. you can't put *any* new words down, irrespective of whether or not they would be adding to something already in-train?

In the case of new ideas, are you exploring all options open to you? In the previous chapter we talked about 'inspiration', where ideas come from. Have you tried the 'active' channels, or are you simply sitting back and waiting for your Muse? If the latter, your "writer's block" might be the result of an unwillingness to go looking for subject matter — and perhaps could be resolved by doing so. Or in more general terms, are you closing yourself off to a world of possibilities? If you are being too specific in what you want to write about — the love-lives of sixteenth century pirates, for example — then you may be tying one writerly hand behind your back. Remind yourself of the 'why' and 'who' that applies to you.

There is *always* something to write about. It doesn't have to be randy pirates!

Sit in a room, look at the walls, the shelves, the tea cup on the table in front of you. Settle on a physical object and ask yourself a question — "I wonder who painted that picture and what their life was like?" or "where did they buy that sculpture?" or "who is that a photograph of?" — and then answer *that* question, write about *that*. Even if only as a 'filler' activity. Who knows what might come of it?

THE TRUTH IS THAT YOU CAN WRITE ABOUT ANYTHING; NO WRITING IS WASTED

Indeed, from the perspective of honing your craft, there is an argument to say that you *should* vary your subject matter from time-to-time, even in pursuit of frivolous 'filler' activity.

So the 'nothing to write about' argument is disqualified. If you are a writer you will find things to write about.

And what is meant by 'unable to produce'? You are only unable to write if it is physically impossible to do so or you have some significant mental impairment — and "writer's block" *doesn't* count as an impairment! Perhaps there is an issue of context in that you are in a situation where you don't have access to pen and paper, or a keyboard, a mobile phone. These are all practical constraints.

Of course you may be unable to write owing to circumstance: you are grieving the loss of a loved one, are going through a divorce, or are in the throes of moving house. These are also valid reasons not to be writing, but a) they are hopefully temporary, and b) they are *not* "writer's block".

Or is 'unable' nothing more than unwillingness? We'll expand on this is "affective component", below.

"creative slowdown" / "unable to produce work for years"

Are you able to measure or contextualise 'slowdown', because 'slow' must surely be in relation to something 'fast'…

Unless you are metronomic — the most extreme version of the structured and methodical writer who produces a thousand words a day, every day, or writes between 10 and 12 o'clock without fail — your writing will inevitably be subject to flux. And to circumstance. So, first question: is what you are experiencing a natural — and temporary — hiatus? Once, when on holiday, I was up early every morning and wrote around 1,800 words. When I returned home and went back to my normal life, did that continue? Of course not! Yet it wasn't a creative slowdown. It was circumstance, context, 'life'.

So, if you are experiencing 'slowdown' is it attributable to other, non-writing factors? If so, then it isn't "writer's block". It's 'living'. And I know what that's like. I had a period where I moved jobs, moved house, got divorced. There were perhaps five or more years when I wrote nothing of substance. At no point did I feel 'blocked'.

But what if nothing material in your life has changed? I was once ploughing on with a novel at a decent enough pace (perhaps 3,000 words a week), but then started to find the work more difficult, hitting the word count harder. It was a 'slowdown' for sure. The reason? I'd fallen out of love with what I was writing; I'd lost belief in the narrative, the characters. The losing of pace was giving me a message about my story — and the one I desperately needed to hear.

I stopped the project.

If you are experiencing difficulty with a specific endeavour and this manifests itself as a 'slowdown' — or even an inability to add any more to it — then ask yourself if you are working on the 'wrong' thing, even if it had once been the 'right' thing. Remember one of our cornerstone questions, the 'what' of writing? Perhaps as a result of circumstance, external factors, or some inner realisation, you are discovering that what you should be writing has changed. It's entirely possible.

So stop. Although abandoning a project in mid-flow can be hard, you should consider doing so (after all, you can always pick it back up at a later date). Don't 'slow down', just stop — and spend your precious time on something different, something more productive and rewarding.

Don't claim you're 'blocked' and give up without rationalising your action (negative); if necessary, make a conscious decision to desist (positive).

And by the way, being able to put something away for a while is a sign of a mature writer.

"affective component"

How does 'mood' play a role — and is it, after all's said and done, the dominant factor?

"Fancy going for a walk?" "How about the gym?" "Do you want to go and see Aunt Henrietta next weekend?" "What about that new Tom Cruise film?"... All of these can — and have been! — answered with the same phrase: "I don't feel like it." Some more than others probably...

But you don't see yourself as a walker, nor an athlete; you've never been that keen on Aunt Henrietta (mainly because of that unfortunate incident in the restaurant a few years ago!), and — to be brutally honest — you don't much care for Tom Cruise either.

There will be times when you don't feel like writing. Many, many times. And that's perfectly natural, acceptable. Even permissible. Or necessary, come to that. But this ennui crosses a line when you choose to label it as "writer's block". That's no more than an excuse for an excuse.

You will hear many professional writers — especially those with established routines — who will profess to writing even when they don't feel like it. Putting words down — even clumsy, inconsequential words that may eventually be thrown away — is essential in order to keep up the heartbeat of being 'a writer'. Yes, the chances are that you're *not* a professional, and your livelihood *isn't* dependant on the next thousand words or the thousand words after that — as much as you might wish it so! — but you're still 'a writer', aren't you?

"I don't feel like it" is hardly a writer's go-to mantra.

THERE ARE TIMES YOU NEED TO OVERRIDE YOUR FEELINGS AND JUST GET ON WITH IT...

More often that I can count (or care to admit), I have not felt like writing — but I have forced myself to sit at my desk, open a file on my computer, and begin. Often such episodes start with a little editing of something recently written; after that I tend to find instinct taking over, and I once again fall into the writing groove. And it doesn't need to be a deep groove: you don't need to slave away for hours on end; sometimes forty minutes is perfectly adequate.

It's a small but important part of the process. I am 'a writer'; that's how I see myself, what I choose to be. And there are consequences of that decision.

...AND A WRITER, WRITES; IF THEY DON'T, THEN WHAT ARE THEY?

Think about 'why' you write — and then if all too often you are prone to 'not feeling like it', perhaps ask yourself whether you're actually a writer at all...

"motivational component"

Although undoubtedly related, there is a subtle difference between the 'affective' and the 'motivational' when it comes to finding excuses not to write: the affective concerns feelings and moods, the motivational is centred more on logic and reason. It can be made concrete. There may be numerous reasons you are suffering from lack of motivation (and therefore choose to label that "writer's block") but the most common complaint is likely to be of the ilk "what's the point?" — and usually with a qualification: "I'll never finish it / I never finish anything", "it will never get published", "it will never make any money", "it's not very good / I'm not good enough / no-one likes it", "we're all going to die anyway"…

Okay that last one's partly tongue-in-cheek, but if you are some flavour of existentialist that's what you might be thinking — which is either an excuse for doing nothing or trying everything, depending on your perspective. And I can't help you with that!

But the others…?

"I'll never finish it / I never finish anything"

This is really a process issue, what 'type' of writer you are. The statement suggests you are unstructured, disorganised, a kind of go-with-the-flow writer who perhaps struggles to find ideas and inspiration too. The first question you need to ask yourself is an easy one: "why do you never finish anything?" Do you get distracted; meander from one project to another; get bored easily; can't see the end point or your way to it; lose faith in your work? These and many others are potential contenders.

Getting to the bottom of your issue is possible but requires individual analysis to do so. However, there are some general things you might consider doing.

1 - Revisit your writing process and see if you can find a more methodical routine for your writing. <u>Ask the 'what type of writer' question again.</u>

2 - Ask yourself whether you have clear line-of-sight to where your project is heading e.g. do you have it mapped out all the way to the end? (Also see the chapter *Planning Z to A* later in this book.)

3 - Try and affirm whether or not you actually *believe* in your project i.e. are you emotionally committed to it, or are you just going through the motions? If the latter, are you prepared to 'throw it away' — metaphorically, that is. And in your heart-of-hearts, is there something else you wish you were working on. <u>Ask the core 'what' question again.</u>

- *"it will never get published"*

If you are talking about getting picked up by Penguin Random House or Simon & Schuster, then sadly this is the reality of the world in which we live. The competition is ridiculously severe; publishers are interested in books that will make them money. That's their business. How many completed novels get picked up by a 'proper' publisher? 1 in 50,000? 1 in 200,000? 1 in 1,000,000? Having said that, your work could still be published via the Indie or self-publishing route (see *Getting Published* towards the end of this book).

But check, is getting published the be-all and end-all? How did you answer the 'why do you write' question? You might need to revisit that; doing so — and potentially reaffirming that something else is more important — could nullify your "it will never get published" complaint.

- *"it will never make any money"*

So that's what it's all about! If that's what is demotivating you, then it should be how you've answered your 'why do I write' question i.e. to make money. Because if you haven't, if you've already identified that there's a more powerful driver than making money, then I can't help but wonder whether or not we're in excuses territory. And if making money is *the* most important thing, then you may have deceived yourself if you answered 'why' any differently.

And a little like the publication complaint above, the very strong chances are that you *won't* make any money. Take those ratios for publishing draft novels and change them by a factor of ten to get a sense of how many people make money writing.

As I've already said, based on various recent surveys (*The Guardian* in 2022, *Publishing Perspectives* in 2023, and others) it seems that the median salary for a published writer is around £7k per annum. For self-published authors it is likely to be a lot less. Obviously there are a few outliers but you shouldn't in all honesty expect to make significant money from writing.

Take poetry. Shifting 300 copies of a collection would make it a 'best seller'. If you're lucky, the poet will make £2 or £3 per copy. Hardly a King's Ransom.

So better to go into writing with the view that you'll never make money — unless you find yourself in a commercial seam of some kind and you're happy to be there.

"it's not very good / I'm not good enough / no-one likes it"

Sadly these may be true — though of course in terms of being 'good' everything's subjective.

We're our own worst critics, either because we're ridiculously harsh on ourselves and therefore *nothing* will ever be good enough, or because we are so self-confident and narcissistic we think everything we produce is sublime. We're not reliable witnesses. It will be the verdict of others which will be the best guide.

So if you can, find someone to give you a view. Don't ask friends or family, you will be putting them in an impossible position to answer honestly: if they say they like it, do they really mean that or are they saying it just because you're their favourite uncle / niece etc.? And if you belong to the kind of writing group where the standard criticism is "that's nice, dear" then don't ask them either! One way or another you have to find a 'beta reader' whose judgement you trust and who you know will be honest — which is harder than you might think. And beware people who ask for money to review your work.

Also hard will be accepting what they say if they are even remotely critical. Being able to take criticism on the chin is a painful lesson that comes with experience. I changed the opening sequence of one novel based on feedback from a beta reader; I wouldn't have been able to do that twenty years ago.

And here's the bottom line: your work may not be good enough. Note: "<u>your work</u>" not "you". This isn't about passing judgement on you as a person — even if your work is intensely personal!

If what you write is not 'good enough' (by whichever measure is meaningful to you) then the subsequent questions are obvious: does it matter? do you carry on? and if you do, with what goals and aspirations? Go back and ask the 'why' and 'who' questions from the standpoint of your new knowledge: they are both vitally important here.

AND RECOGNISE THAT, ALTHOUGH YOU MAY NOT BE 'A WRITER', IT DOESN'T STOP YOU FROM WRITING

THE QUESTIONS YOU NEED TO ASK YOURSELF...

If you think you're suffering from "writer's block" then the first question is 'Are you? Really?!' And if your answer is a categorical 'yes', then you <u>must</u> to try to define and make it concrete, break it down and explain — to yourself of course! — exactly what you mean. How does this 'block' manifest itself?

If relevant, you can use the subdivisions above — 'unable to produce new work', 'creative slowdown' etc. — to scope out your issue, and then delve a little deeper by asking yourself the related questions. I don't for one minute claim they're comprehensive, but they may help; you may find that one of them unlocks something, allows you to say "ah, maybe *that's* it..."

...AND THINGS TO TRY

Some people wear "writer's block" like a badge of honour: it both allows them to claim to be a writer *and* excuses them from the hard graft of writing. Maximum benefit, minimum effort.

Most don't, of course. For most people — those who desperately want to write — "writer's block" is an affliction, a curse, a blemish on their writerly soul. And yet if you really want to write, then find a way to do so; find something new to write about — or somewhere new to write; location is often important. Unless you are practically or emotionally prevented from doing so, you have no excuse!

Because here's the $64,000 question:

WHAT IF YOU'RE NOT REALLY A WRITER AT ALL, AND "WRITER'S BLOCK" IS IN FACT A DEMONSTRATION OF THAT?

There is no litmus test to prove definitively, one way or the other, whether we are writers. Inevitably there's a spectrum. At one end (the alkali?) we have those who, we would all agree, are writers. Like Shakespeare. At the other, more 'acidic' end, the many millions of people who have never written in their lives — like my late Aunt Gladys. And in between, the rest of us, not only trying to find our place on the continuum but also endeavouring to edge a little closer to the Bard and a little further away from dear Gladys.

And who's to say where our rightful place is? There are those people who argue that "if you write, you're a writer"; others who demand a degree of competence or evidence of output (however slim that canon might be); and others still who say that you can only call yourself a writer if that's how you earn your living, if that's what is says on your passport as 'profession'.

We'll all have a view.

What I think is indisputable though is the need to prove that the activity has been undertaken, income and quality and volume aside. Earning nothing or earning a great deal is not proof that you are a good or bad writer. Similarly, writing three books a year doesn't mean you're 'good' either.

But not writing? Choosing to <u>not</u> pick up your pen nor open your keyboard and the word processing software to which it gives you access, and *then* claiming "writer's block" is, I would argue, evidence against the defendant.

A cyclist cycles; a knitter knits; a swimmer swims — why should the criteria for a writer be any different? Because we're 'special'?

I don't think so.

IMPOSTER SYNDROME

Many writers are wracked with a strange internal dilemma: they are sure there is something unique and special about their work, while at the same time believe it isn't really 'good enough'. It's like having two voices inside your head constantly fighting for attention, both claiming primacy and that they know best.

Of course others are highly ego-centric, brimming with self-belief, even annoying arrogance. They have managed (publicly at least!) to banish the nay-saying voice — assuming there might have been one nagging at them in the first place! Simply because such people have unshakeable self-confidence doesn't mean their writing is *that* good; in fact, it might not be better than ours. Indeed, it might be terrible! The same is true of best-sellers.

> JUST BECAUSE SOMETHING SELLS LOTS OF COPIES AND MAKES TONS OF MONEY, DOESN'T NECESSARILY MEAN IT IS WELL-WRITTEN

The majority of writers are at the 'humble' end of the spectrum, constantly assailed by both voices, more inclined to believe the nay-sayer than the one telling them their work is good.

Is this a scenario you recognise?

The label most commonly applied to this self-doubt is Imposter Syndrome. Yet what is 'Imposter Syndrome'?

- "Impostor syndrome is a psychological occurrence in which an individual doubts their skills, talents, or accomplishments and has a persistent fear of being exposed as a fraud." — *Wikipedia*

Ring any bells? I'm sure you'll recognise it if you feel you're a slave to Imposter Syndrome!

Putting the work itself to one side, what are the symptoms?

- You are self-deprecating about your work in public, often making excuses or apologising for it.
- You try and create a buffer by saying that something is 'in draft' or 'a work-in-progress' because you worry that by saying something is 'finished' or that you really like it might be the equivalent of saying "this is the limit of my abilities".
- Whilst praising others' work, secretly you feel it is inferior to yours — the point here being that you are so insecure in your own achievements that you refrain from honest criticism, adopting a defence mechanism in preference to hinting at your superiority.
- Perhaps you struggle to complete individual projects, assailed by uncertainty and insecurity. The "what's the point?" question is never far away.

And so on. You probably have your own examples, and maybe — if not those above — your own symptoms.

I suspect there are two main responses to the notion of Imposter Syndrome. The first is that it doesn't exist, and is more likely to be an excuse for laziness, for not putting the work in. The second — almost certainly endorsed by its sufferers — is that Imposter Syndrome is 'a bad thing'.

Unlike "writer's block", I believe Imposter Syndrome *does* exist — mainly because I suffer from it. Less than in the past I'll admit, but that nagging voice is an ever-present.

But a universally 'bad thing'? I'm not so sure.

IT MAY BE POSSIBLE TO EMBRACE IMPOSTER SYNDROME AND TURN IT TO YOUR ADVANTAGE

But how?

If we assume that the underlying message we're giving ourselves (because that's where it comes from; it's *internal*) is that our work isn't good enough, you *could* choose to reframe the complaint by saying 'it could be better'. And it could be. Always. Can you imagine what it would be like to write something so perfect that you could never reach those dizzy heights again? Every writing day would be a disappointment. Every day. You would constantly strive to replicate your triumph — and constantly feel you were failing. Surely that would be torture.

But never fear, writing something that's perfect is impossible!

If we choose to tell ourselves "that piece of work is okay, but it could be better", we turn Imposter Syndrome into a force which can drive us forwards. But this only really works if we can avoid indulging in all that self-effacing nonsense — which, if our work is actually half-decent, is only likely to alienate those who admire it. After all, what does it say about our readers if they like something that's been labelled 'rubbish' by it's author?!

To a certain extent at least part of this argument is superficial; it doesn't get to the heart of the matter. Indeed, I would argue that one key source of Imposter Syndrome is a writer's failure to understand themselves 'as a writer'.

IMPOSTER SYNDROME IS FAR MORE LIKELY TO AFFECT PEOPLE WHO DON'T PROPERLY UNDERSTAND THEIR 'WHY', 'WHO', 'TYPE' & 'WHAT'

After all, Imposter Syndrome is the expression of a lack of confidence as much as it's the doubting of talent.

I knew a man who was writing a novel (his first) and he was supremely confident in it. He knew why he was writing it, who he was writing it for, what type of writer he was, and also the entirety of the 'what': structure, plan, etcetera. There wasn't an ounce of Imposter Syndrome in him — even though his writing was average at best. How could he be an impostor if he knew exactly what he was doing and why he was doing it?

Sometimes Imposter Syndrome has nothing to do with quality.

So when you're considering Imposter Syndrome — what it is, whether you suffer from it, and so on — be sure to look at it in the round. Claiming you suffer from it without actually considering what that *means* is akin to claiming to be a 'pantser' who can't produce a plan — when you've never actually tried to do so.

But there is one further important thought. And it's not a positive one.

YOU MAY SUFFER FROM IMPOSTER SYNDROME SIMPLY BECAUSE YOU ARE AN IMPOSTER

You don't write well. Your work is substandard, clumsy, juvenile, clichéd, unoriginal. You have no sense of rhythm or tempo; you have no sensitivity in terms of language or syntax.

And quite possibly you see none of those failings.

THE QUESTIONS YOU NEED TO ASK YOURSELF...

So how can you get to grips with Imposter Syndrome? How can you establish whether or not you have it — and if you do, what you might do to release yourself from its clutches? And what if, at the end of all your investigations and soul-searching you still believe you *are* an imposter? What then?

Perhaps the first thing to do is to revisit the initial four questions with which we started this whole exploration: 'why do you write?', 'who are you writing for?', 'what type of writer are you?', and 'what are you writing?'. The reason for this is simple. If you have told yourself you are writing for a particular combination of why/who/type and this simply is not who you are as a writer, then it would be entirely feasible for you to feel you were suffering from Imposter Syndrome on the basis that you might *never* be able to meet your unrealistic expectations.

For example, let's say that you are writing a treatise or manifesto, a work of non-fiction which you believe will change how people view contemporary politics. That may be what you are trying to do, but what if you don't have the depth of experience and knowledge to produce something that is suitably informed and credible? What if there is nothing original in your ideas? Or what if no-one is interested in what you are saying or you don't have a platform? Under those circumstances, how could you not feel an imposter?

If any one of 'why', 'who', 'type' or 'what' is misaligned with who you really are as a writer — and, in consequence, you are striving to achieve something that may be impossible — Imposter Syndrome will never be far away. After all, that "persistent fear of being exposed as a fraud" clearly speaks to being unable to achieve your goals. If I make a claim to be training for a slot on the athletics team for the next Olympic Games, how can I not be a fraud given my best times at my chosen distance are double the current qualification time — never mind that I don't belong to an athletics club and am too old to be competitive!

But wait. You *are* writing a political treatise — the words are pouring out of you! — and I *am* in training, running five times a week. So still impostors then? If you tweak either the 'why' or the 'who' of your motivation — for example, realise you are writing the manifesto for yourself, or are undertaking the training simply in order to get fit — then the major reason for feeling an imposter vanishes. Once again we see the power of those four initial questions...and of getting them aligned.

What else might you ask yourself?

Are you too self-deprecating, too modest and self-effacing? Do you fail to stand up for your work, even when you believe it to be good?

> You will feel less like an imposter when you start to publicly believe in what you are doing.

Are you too reserved when it comes to critiquing others' efforts? Do you worry that your views will not be taken seriously?

> Offering constructive criticism is in part sourced from the belief that you know enough about your craft (and therefore your own work) to possess the wherewithal to offer an opinion — and that others see and believe it too. If you belong to one, think about how criticism works in your writing group: who are the people most listened to and why? And in terms of their relationship to their writing, how does it differ from yours?

Have you failed to complete anything worthwhile, and as a result do you believe you haven't the credentials to consider yourself a writer and therefore don't qualify to offer criticism?

> If that is the case, have you ever attempted to define why it is you've never finished anything, because the issue may well be elsewhere and nothing to do with Imposter Syndrome.

...AND THINGS TO TRY

How you answer the questions above may well prompt things for you to try, not only in relation to the why/who/type/what of writing, but also from the perspective of your persona, having a greater degree of self-belief, altering how you behave with other people, your approach to criticism etcetera.

Obviously you cannot flick a switch on your personality; if you are terribly introverted you aren't going to suddenly become an extrovert — but recognition of how you behave can help you to manage your interactions with others.

~

But what if you really are an imposter? How can you know? The only valid measure is, I think, the opinion of others. Getting this relies on two factors: first, finding people you trust and whose opinion you value; and second, asking them the hard questions and persuading them to be honest. "What do you think about this poem / chapter etc.?" is an easy enough question to ask — and also one where a truthful answer might be easily ducked. If you go down this route, your questioning will need to be as explicit as you can possibly make it.

And if your work simply isn't very good, if you are 'last among equals' in your group, what then? Are you ready to receive that kind of feedback?

JUST BECAUSE YOU WRITE DOESN'T MAKE YOU A WRITER, IN THE SAME WAY THAT OCCASIONALLY PAINTING OR DRAWING DOESN'T MAKE YOU AN ARTIST

In simple terms you can choose to stop trying to be a writer — or **modify what being a writer means for you**. Go back to the 'why' and the 'who' and redefine those in the context of your laid-bare reality.

Does this mean that you're not a writer? *In the sense in which you hoped and intended to be one*, perhaps yes. How can it not? But based on a revised profile..?

'PLANNER' OR 'PANTSER'?

It won't surprise you to know that I spent a fair amount of time planning this book: choosing the topics, setting out the sequence in which I would tackle them, deciding what would go into each chapter. How else could you produce a volume such as this?

In many people's view there are two kinds of writer: those who plan — the 'planners' — and those who are proud to do no such thing, who 'wing it' and plan nothing — the 'pantsers'. There is a subset of those (in both camps) who wear their label like a badge of honour and deride those from the 'other side', feigning an inability to comprehend how one can possibly work in such a way!

Yet as with so many sets of opposites, 'planners' and 'pantsers' are actually on the same spectrum, and not only can you occupy any point on this spectrum, you can sit at various locations on it *simultaneously*. The two are *not* mutually exclusive, nor is a writer likely to be 100% one or the other.

MOST OF US ARE A BLEND OF 'PLANNER' AND 'PANTSER'

If you are writing a work of non-fiction it is more likely that you will need to approach it from a planner's perspective: there will be research to be carried out, facts to check; the way the book is laid out will need to support your facts and research in the most effective manner possible. You simply can't go weaving about all over the place. Can you imagine an important chronological series of events told in a haphazard fashion?

On the other hand, if you are writing poetry then — putting aside the practicalities of compiling a collection — you are likely to be driven by the moment, by instinct, by emotion. How can you possibly 'plan' a poem, other than perhaps in the structural sense? "I'm going to write a sonnet" perhaps.

And fiction? Probably somewhere in-between; after all, the plot needs to hang together doesn't it, and for it to do so convincingly and comprehensively surely some planning *must* be needed. My experience tells me this needs to be done relatively early on in the process, but I have heard of people who plough on to the end of their first draft plan-less and then go back to try and find — and hopefully fix! — all the holes and inconsistencies. I'm not saying that's wrong (there is no 'wrong', remember?) but surely not the most efficient approach.

All of which means that if you are someone who works in multiple genres — fiction and poetry being the most likely combination I suspect — then you may find yourself occupying different positions on the aforementioned spectrum at the same time.

However, the truth of the matter is that one way or another we are all 'pantsers'. If you take the term to mean someone who doesn't know what is coming next, then every time we draft something, put one word in front of another — in *any* genre — we are doing so with no foreknowledge as to which word will come next. If, by definition, a 'planner' <u>knows</u> that A follows B follows C, then when you are drafting you *cannot* possibly be a 'planner'. Yes, you have planned to write something about a walk in the woods, describing the path, the undergrowth etcetera, but how do you <u>know</u> which adjective you will use between 'the' and 'tree' until you have written it? In that sense, via the logic of it, we're all 'pantsers'.

Yet common usage of the two terms simplifies their meaning when it comes to creative writing: a 'pantser' never knows what's coming next, a 'planner' always does. What does your badge say?

Actually you've already started to answer that one.

The question 'what type of writer are you?' began to tease at it. Indeed two of the suggested answers were 'go with the flow' and 'structured and methodical'. At the time we were talking about your generic approach to the *process* of writing: regular targets, regular writing slots etcetera. But 'what type of writer are you?' can apply to your writing methodology equally well. And, believe it or not, the two halves of your answer might not be in synch. You might, for example, be methodical in that you sit down to write from 4-to-5 p.m. every day — yet when you do so you have no idea what you are going to write e.g. what happens next in the story you are crafting. Alternatively, you may have planned out your novel in the nth degree, but simply have no idea when you will do any work on it because it all depends on how you 'feel'.

We have arrived at yet another example of no 'right' answers, as well as further demonstration that knowing yourself is of critical importance in making the most of your talent.

SUCCESS IS PARTLY ABOUT UNDERSTANDING YOUR PROCESS AND HOW YOU WRITE – AND THEN BUILDING YOUR WORKING MODEL AROUND THAT

In my own case I often start a story with no idea what it is, what it will be about, nor how long it will be. Or even if I'll end up completing it at all! I will be a 'pantser' for a while, letting the narrative develop and take me along. Then if it appears I may have landed on something which feels as if it needs many thousands more words to resolve, I will take a step back from it — usually at around 8,000-12,000 words. At this point I become a 'planner': I think about plot threads, character profiles, timelines, and so forth; I start to turn my vague meanderings into something more solid and concrete. For me this is a vital stage in the process; it allows me to see my way through the story, assess whether or not it has potential, and — most importantly of all —

whether or not I 'believe' in it. If it all looks good enough, I go back to my story, working through the framework I have built while planning. If not, then I will have no hesitation in considering abandoning the endeavour.

I'm not saying this is the way to work, only that it's *my* process for fiction — especially long-form fiction. It's a process refined after many years of trial and error.

THE QUESTIONS YOU NEED TO ASK YOURSELF...AND THINGS TO TRY

So what questions should you ask yourself? Is it as simple as identifying whether or not you are a 'planner' or a 'pantser' — or accepting that you are actually both?

Well, such recognition is certainly a good place to start — and it should be a simple question to answer. If you don't know instinctively — and I'm sure you will! — then you only need to look at your notebooks, your drafts, your files, to see whether there are any spreadsheets or other documents which outline timelines, chapter breakdowns, character profiles etcetera. Or if there are none.

As I've said before, if you write non-fiction I would expect the 'planner' side of the scales to be as low as it will go, with the opposite being true for poets. For writers of fiction, in whatever form, you are probably a blend. Don't worry about whether or not the scales are in balance (i.e. you are at the mid-point on the spectrum), that's irrelevant: knowing your profile, understanding yourself, is what's key.

Then, having done this, return to the 'what type of writer are you?' question in order to triangulate. Finding a clear misalignment should prompt you to think about making some changes. But what kind of changes?

- ***Process / Approach***

    If you're a 'pantser' when it comes to putting words together, but are a structured and methodical person, then either allow yourself to work within a looser structure, or try to step back from your work and see if you are able to think ahead a little more, plan the next phase of work — even if you simply start with an idea of what you'll do tomorrow.

    Alternatively, if you are super-relaxed about when you work but insist on having a really detailed plan to work to, then try and introduce more structure into when you actually sit down and write.

- ***What***

    Your only other variable is what you are working on. As we've already said, it is entirely possible that where you are on the 'planner-pantser' spectrum is incompatible with what you are writing. If that is the case, in addition to trying to adjust either process or approach, you might want to revalidate that you are actually writing the most appropriate thing given your profile — and given how you answered 'why' and 'who'

These are obviously only suggestions offered from the perspective of trying to ensure you maximise your talent, and harmonise the 'why', 'who', 'type' and 'what' of your writing life.

NO-ONE CAN TELL YOU WHAT COMBINATION WILL WORK

Practice, trial and error, learning about your writing persona; these are all within your control — and you should commit to aligning those as best you can if you truly want to become the best writer you can be.

PLANNING - Z TO A

There are several reasons why you may find planning difficult:

- It doesn't come naturally to you i.e. you have always been more of a 'pantser'; that's simply how you roll.
- You find the mechanics of it too hard; you think you *can* plan (or you know you *should* plan) but you don't really know *how* to go about it.
- The process aspects of planning is not the issue; you simply find it difficult to look ahead.

We covered the 'planner' versus 'pantser' clash in the previous chapter, so here we'll look at planning mechanics and projecting forwards.

But before we do that, a home truth: **time is the most precious and finite resource we have** — and we've no idea how much of it will be at our disposal. Which makes this all the more significant:

A DAY LOST...IS A DAY LOST

If you choose not to write one Monday then you won't get that opportunity back. Ever. This is not to say that you must write every day, far from it; rather it is a plea to recognise that there is a 'cost' of not doing so, or a balance to be struck with how you spend you time. Writing aside, being content and happy is probably the primary goal to which we should all aim, and this may or may not involve writing on that particular Monday.

My only aim here is to emphasise how important our time is — and from that to extrapolate that 'spending' it wisely is important. One way to ensure we get the most from that precious commodity is to know — as best as we possibly can — the shape and destination of what we are working on i.e. to have a plan.

"YOU CAN'T SPEND TIME TWICE"[5]

A plan can revolve around how we spend our time and when we write, as well as the route we need to take to get from A to Z on our work-in-progress.

We've already touched on the former in the chapter concerning how you identify what type of writer you are i.e. being structured in trying to be clear on *when* you are going to write and *how much* you are going to try and write (hours or words etc.).

Here I am going to focus on the planning as it relates to *what* you are writing, and will touch on both the mechanics of planning, and mapping out how you might envision getting to the end of a project.

The mechanics of planning

If a plan describes how an end goal is achieved — such as arriving at a destination or building something — it is essentially not much more than a visual representation of the steps between where you are ('A') and where you want to get to ('Z'). These plans can be entirely graphical — for example, the instructions for putting together a piece of Ikea furniture — or highly technical — such as a Gantt chart for a complex infrastructure project.

From a writing perspective, in most cases our plans will take the form of a list of some kind. Indeed, that may be the easiest way to think about them. Often, when people go shopping, they write out their shopping list on the basis of the store's configuration: the fruit and vegetables are nearest the entrance so they go at the

---

[5] from *Crash - the last 30 minutes of a life* - Ian Gouge, Coverstory books, 2023

top of the list; the wines and spirits at the far end of the store, so they go at the bottom. The objective is to put together an efficient list i.e. so that you don't keep doubling back on yourself as you shop *and* you don't miss anything.

Putting together a plan for a writing project — be it the compilation of a collection of poems or the drafting of a play — is not really much different: you want your plan to be accurate, effective, and to miss nothing out. You know you need to produce a final draft, but you are not going to do that before the first edit is complete; you may need some back cover blurb, but you probably want to produce an outline of the whole cover first — layouts for front and back — to know what space is available. And so forth.

PLANNING IS LITTLE MORE THAN THE APPLICATION OF RUDIMENTARY LOGIC

So think of a plan as not much more than a list. How you manifest that list is probably the one thing many people find difficult.

It doesn't need to be sophisticated. Just a list will be fine, if that's how your mind works; and scribbled on a piece of paper could be good enough. Thanks to computers, these days we are spoiled for choice in terms of tools available to us: word processing software, spreadsheets, 'mind-maps', specialist planning tools, and so forth.

There is no 'best' way. As with so much in our writing process, whatever works for you is the way to go. And again, trial and error will be required to land on what that might be. In my own case I will use a spreadsheet for complex planning, such as the plot and timelines of a novel; yet for other things — like this book! — I find a detailed breakdown in a word processing document perfectly adequate. I have tried 'mind-maps' in the past but they simply don't work for me.

What you choose will also depend on how 'tech-savvy' you are. The advantage of using software is, of course, that your plans will be easy to modify and keep up-to-date.

✣ *Working out how you get from A to Z*

In order to create a plan you need to know what the steps are i.e. the items on your shopping list. Some writers find this the more difficult aspect of planning. You know, logically, that your plan must break down the overall task into the steps between 'A' and 'Z'; and you also know that 'B' should follow 'A', 'C' follow 'B', and so forth. This challenge is most typically relevant to the plotting of a long work of fiction, though not exclusively so.

The first difficulty can arise in trying to understand how many steps there are between 'A' and 'Z': 26? 15? 120? And secondary to identifying all these is having the confidence that you have them in the correct sequence i.e. one which allows your novel to flow and make sense to the reader. For example, mid-drafting you may realise that it should be 'B-D-C' and not 'B-C-D'; how you manifest your plan should let you accommodate such changes.

However, one fundamental element in all of this which is often missed — and which consequently makes planning harder — is being absolutely clear that you know what 'A' and 'Z' represent.

At the macro level, part of 'A' will be your answers to the 'why' and 'who' questions; at the micro level it will be how you see the 'what': the first the pages of your story, the opening scene, its location, characters, action etc.

Once you have 'A', the next logical step would seem to be to identify what happens in 'B', then 'C' and so on. Part of the challenge with this approach is that, if unverified, you might find your narrative 'wanders around' lacking focus. And secondly — and more fundamentally — you may discover that you simply *don't know* what comes next i.e. what on earth happens in 'E'?! It can be more difficult than you might imagine to move yourself and your characters forward incrementally, chronologically, and coherently.

One reason for this could be that you have not yet defined what 'Z' looks like i.e. how will the story end? And when I say 'story', it could be a novel, a novella or short story, a play, non-fiction, or even a collection of poetry where there is a logical journey of some kind.

But let's stick with long-form fiction for now. Do you know what happens in the end? Is the murderer revealed? Are the lovers reunited? Is the 'big question' answered? If you think about Booker's seven plots, each of these will have a 'typical' ending e.g. the journey is completed (or not), the quest is successful (or not), and so forth. The importance in knowing what 'Z' looks like is that it gives you a bookend to your story; more importantly, you know where you are heading. Not only will this help prevent your narrative from 'meandering', it can also provide you with a good place to *start* planning — as illogical as that might sound.

For example. Your main character, Adele, is in both 'A' and 'Z', but the Adele at the end of the narrative will inevitably be different in some way: she will have learned things, done things, experienced things. Knowing Adele both 'before' and 'after' — a potential by-product of the character profile (see the next chapter) — allows you to ask yourself the question "what *needs* to happen to Adele between 'A' and 'Z' in order to make the ending effective and believable, and her whole journey coherent?" And the answer will be a list: she needs to meet Jim, she needs to shoot Bob, she needs to run away to Canada, and so on. Each of these elements in Adele's journey from 'A' to 'Z' are essentially plot points in the story. You can go through the same exercise for Jim, Bob, and all your other characters. What you will end up with is a comprehensive list of all the things that *must* happen — not what you are *guessing* happens. And it will be a list of action points that are all heading in the same direction. There is no 'meandering about'; you will have avoided "what shall I do with Jim now?" because you *know* what has to happen to him; and you are less likely to write something that is irrelevant in terms of the progression of the overall narrative.

Once you have your list of plot points, then planning is all about putting them in the correct sequence in which they need to appear, the journey from 'A' to 'Z'. Nothing more, nothing less — just like that shopping list. Suddenly you have a plan!

This is only one approach of course, one little trick which might help you along the way.

SOMETIMES STARTING AT THE END CAN BE THE BEST WAY TO BEGIN!

THE QUESTIONS YOU NEED TO ASK YOURSELF...AND THINGS TO TRY

I would suggest you revisit the key points in this chapter in relation to a specific project or work-in-progress, especially if there is one with which you are having difficulty.

1. Make sure you understand how you write i.e. are you a 'planner' or a 'pantser'? Where on the spectrum do you sit?
2. What impact (if any) do you think this is having on the work in focus?
3. Do you have a plan for your w-i-p — and if you do, is it *really* driving your project forward? After all, having a plan is one

thing, but it is only a 'good' plan if it is facilitating progress towards achieving the end-goal. If it's not a good plan, is that a failure in the list of steps (i.e. it's not detailed or comprehensive enough) or in the way you have constructed it (i.e. it's just a random sequence of plot points)?

4. If you have put together plans in the past and none of them worked, consider whether or not you were using the best method / tool (a carry forward from the previous question). And what was distinctive about those plans that *did* work?

5. Are you unsure about the detailed breakdown of your plan? If you have never used a spreadsheet, for example, there are lots of example formats you can download from the internet. The same is true of tools like 'mind-maps'; free software is available.

6. Honing in on the writing *project* rather than the planning *process*, do you know what both 'A' and 'Z' look like, the start and the end? (At this stage you don't need to worry whether you have the 'right' 'A' and/or 'Z' because these can easily be changed during the editing process.) If you don't understand either bookend well enough, spend some time trying to define them a little better. Remember, 'A' <u>initiates</u> the action, and 'Z' brings it to some kind of <u>conclusion</u>.

7. When you have both 'A' and 'Z' defined, have a go at backward planning, character by character. See what you come up with in terms of a list of plot points. When I have my list, often I write each plot point on a 3x5 or 4x6 index card (one card per plot point, the cards often colour-coded e.g. yellow ones relate to Adele, blue ones to Jim). Once I have all the cards written out I can then manually re-sequence them until I arrive at a progression and flow which suits both the narrative and the construct of the novel — and

it becomes far easier to get a feel of what A-E-C-D-F-B looks like versus A-B-C-D-E-F or any other combination.

WHEN IT COMES TO PLANNING, NEVER UNDER-ESTIMATE THE POWER OF A HAND-WRITTEN 3X5 INDEX CARD!

As I've said before, this is just one approach. Although it has worked for me, it may not for you. But never fear, there are lots of other approaches; the internet will be awash with suggestions around planning.

Oh, and don't fall into the trap of saying "I'm a 'pantser', I never plan!" Not only is that lazy thinking, but you may be doing yourself and your craft a disservice.

You may just need to try out a few planning approaches to find the one that works for you...

THE IMPORTANCE OF CHARACTER PROFILES

For the writers of narrative-based work — fiction or plays — there is a fundamental 'chicken or egg' conundrum:

WHAT COMES FIRST: PLOT OR CHARACTER?

You will probably have a view. It's the kind of binary question about which strong opinions may well be expressed! And — as ever — neither answer will be incorrect; it all depends how you work. I once met a scriptwriter who was strongly of the opinion that you must begin with people: "everything starts with the characters". Perhaps the writer of complex murder-mysteries might disagree...

But what do we mean by 'character' anyway? A couple of definitions to get us started (with my emphasis):

- "The character of a person or place consists of <u>*all the qualities*</u> they have that make them <u>*distinctive*</u> from other people or places." - Collins Dictionary

  ○ Characters need to be distinctive in order a) to differentiate them from one and other, and b) for them to be realistic. One having blue eyes and another brown is **not** *meaningful* distinctiveness.

  ○ Quite rightly the emphasis is on "all the qualities" — and the most important ones are those you cannot see.

  ○ Interestingly this definition suggests both person *and* place are relevant when it comes to character, or perhaps more accurately 'characteristics' — and you can see why. Describe London and then describe a small town in the country; both will have multiple schools, churches, shops, houses of various shapes and sizes, yet the character of the small town will be radically different to London — and not merely because of scale.

- "A character is a person, animal, being, creature, or thing in a story. Writers use characters to *perform the actions* and *speak dialogue, moving the story along a plot line*." - literaryterms.net
  - Again a definition which suggests that we should look beyond people when thinking about character: Woody in the *Toy Story* movies, perhaps; the animals in *Animal Farm*…
  - Characters are the active components in narrative; they 'perform the actions' and 'speak dialogue', 'moving the story along a plot line'. If they do none of those things, we should ask ourselves why they are there.

In broad terms, **plot** is *static* and generally linear (because time is linear, however we choose to write our story), but **characters** should always be *dynamic*. Even our examples of London and a sleepy country town are dynamic, always moving, ever changing — though to different degrees!

Overall we might argue that

PLOT IS THE FRAMEWORK; CHARACTERS ARE FLUID

Characters are what make our plot come alive; their contribution makes it successful, coherent, believable — and therefore the characters themselves must also be coherent and believable.

CHARACTERS PROPEL THE PLOT FORWARD; THE ACTION OF THE PLOT CHANGES CHARACTERS

But what if you don't understand your characters well enough or early enough on the writing journey? How can you possibly know how they are going to behave, both to move the story along as well as when interacting with each other?

Here's a simple example.

Imagine a conversation between these two:

In this example — the UK's King Charles III and former US President Donald Trump — you could probably make a decent fist of conjuring a dialogue, especially if you live in North America or Western Europe; after all, you are likely to know something about both of these men. And interestingly, if I were to ask you to highlight their dominant characteristics, it is almost certain that you would _not_ focus on their height, hair or eye colour etcetera, but on their personalities, what they believed in or represented.

And now imagine a conversation between the two people below.

Where do you start?! Unless you happened to be related to one of them or are their friend you will have no idea who they are; two anonymous faces plucked from the internet. In order to fabricate a conversation between them you would need to make assumptions about age, beliefs, professions, background, hopes and dreams, histories etc. Again, the length or colour of hair etcetera is almost entirely irrelevant.

The point of this example is to demonstrate that the 'seen' is less important than you might imagine. Eye colour, body shape and so forth are all 'easy' attributes; whether a character has blue or brown eyes will (in the vast majority of instances) make no material difference to your story. The exercise also proves how the 'unseen' attributes drive a character's contribution to the narrative — emotions, history, prejudice, flaws, strengths etc.

REMEMBER: "THE CHARACTER OF A PERSON OR PLACE CONSISTS OF <u>ALL</u> THE QUALITIES THEY HAVE THAT MAKE THEM <u>DISTINCT</u> FROM OTHER PEOPLE"

If there is a temptation to shortcut character outlining, the end-result may be fictional characters are *not* unique; many will end up as cheap imitations of real / known people, film / TV characters, or fit some kind of popular stereotype. It can be all too easy to do this without realising it. For example, if you say "he's my Trump character" then most likely you will end up with a poor imitation of some populist vision of the ex-President.

So how can we avoid this? How do we create 'rounded' and complex characters that a) will be unique and b) do what they need to do in terms of progressing our story?

The answer lies in the character profile.

So what is a 'character profile'? Essentially it's a list: a series of attributes, characteristics, elements of personal history and narrative-specific components which, combined together, go to make up a pen-portrait of the individual about whom you are writing. The profiles can be as in-depth as you choose to make them and will, to a certain extent, be driven by the nature of the story you are telling — but it is important that they are <u>consistent</u> across all the characters involved in the story i.e. one template for all the actors in a single narrative.

Coming up with a profile is a two step process: first, you define your template; second, you then complete the profile for each of your characters. Before taking you through the method, an illustration as to how powerful this tool can be.

I was at an early stage in writing *Once Significant Others* and had drafted around 11,000 words when I ran into difficulty. I had introduced the six main characters and had the whole of the novel planned out — and yet for some reason I was unable to get traction on the next section of the book where the characters started to interact with each other.

Steven Nesbit, playwright and screenwriter (*A Very British Christmas* [2019], *Gloves Off* [2017], *North v South* [2015]), asked me how well I knew my characters; he wondered whether I might be stuck because I didn't know them well enough. Steve is undoubtedly in the 'character first' camp! He suggested I consider defining them more fully before carrying on. So I spent some time drawing up and then completing a profile for each. There were around thirty elements in the template.

One of the questions in the profile was "What was their childhood like?"

To this day I've no idea why I included this; it wasn't something at all relevant to the plot, yet instinctively I'd added it in. I considered deleting the question or giving myself the option not to answer it, but in the end I answered every question for every character.

In the main section of the novel my cast are having dinner. During the scene, one of them says something to which I found another could respond in a manner that was *driven by her experience of childhood*. If I had not included that question in the profile, she would never have been able to do that. Moreover, because I knew the childhood background for <u>all</u> the characters, I was able to add in a brief childhood-related exchange initiated by that first response. It only lasted a few lines, but it allowed me to demonstrate the characters as rounded, make the whole scene more realistic. If I hadn't attempted the profile, I would never have included this small but important fragment in the book.

In summary, my stepping away from the draft to complete the profiles completely unlocked the writing process.

...AND THINGS TO TRY

Well, there really is only one; and though I'm focussing here on long-form fiction, the process works equally well for a play or screenplay, novellas, and potentially even short stories.

Choose a work-in-progress or a project you are thinking of starting, one where you appreciate how a comprehensive understanding of your characters will benefit the end product. Then do as follows:

1. Download / print some profile examples from the internet — e.g. by searching for 'character profiles' or something similar. You should ignore any which only cover the 'easy' physical attributes.

2. From those you have found, curate your own template, most likely in Word or Excel (or equivalent). I would recommend you avoid just using the first profile you find. By creating your

own template you will be more invested in it, and you can fine-tune it to fit your w-i-p.

3. Include all the elements — seen and unseen — that are likely to be relevant to your plot. For example, a murder mystery is likely to highlight some different components in your characters' make-up compared to Sci-Fi or Romance or Family Saga e.g. 'motive'.

4. Review the list to ensure it is suitable and thorough. Tip: some questions should strike you as 'difficult' to answer — that's a good sign! Perhaps use yourself as a test-case: if the completed profile described you, how good a picture would that give someone?

5. For each relevant / major character, force yourself to answer **all** elements of the profile. This is because you need to know them equally well, and because doing so will give you the most 'hooks' and opportunities when writing.

6. Once finished, become familiar with the people you have created i.e. review and refine the profiles you have produced. If you have already started drafting, go back and revisit what you have written thus far and edit in the light of the new knowledge you have of them.

7. Keep the profiles handy (printed out or on-screen) when you are writing.

I would be stunned if making this effort didn't result in your characters being more realistic and believable, and improve the quality of your output.

A SAMPLE CHARACTER PROFILE

Here is a list of some of the elements I settled on for the profiles in *Once Significant Others*. Given it's a very character-heavy and action-light novel, these were priceless.

Note how so very few of them relate to the 'easy' elements of an individual's character:

This should give you an idea as to how to pull together a character profile and what it could contain. Good luck!

DoB / Age	Significant moments that changed their life
Occupation	Who or what do they love most
Relevant Family info	Who or what do they hate most
Appearance at first glance	What do they believe in
How do they speak	What quirks do they have
Basic need / want to be fulfilled in the story	What is the most impressive thing about them
Relationship history	What is the worst thing they have ever done
Character flaw	What do they need to achieve in relation to your plot
Character strength	How can you show this
What other people see in them	What specific plot points and incidents need to be written
What is important to them	Do they have any backstory related to the plot / themes
What was their childhood like	Who are they close to
What are they hiding	What changes in their personality and circumstances will be effected by the end of the novel

DIALOGUE VS. MONOLOGUE

In any form of fiction although the role of dialogue is crucial, it can be under-utilised or realised ineffectively. Writers may be tempted to rush through the drafting of dialogue without giving it too much care and attention — after all, it's just people talking, isn't it?

Closely associated with dialogue is the monologue, that powerful single-voiced and intensely personal observation of the world. Yet here too writers can fall into another trap i.e. treating monologue as if it were just the same as dialogue, not appreciating the difference between the two.

BOTH DIALOGUE AND MONOLOGUE ARE IMMENSELY POWERFUL TOOLS, OFTEN NOT UTILISED TO THE FULL

Before we take a look at the two *distinct* forms, what do we mean by 'dialogue' and 'monologue'? Let's start with some definitions (with my emphasis); accurate or not, these can be useful to provoke discussion:

- "Dialogue: <u>conversation</u> written for a book, play, or film" - Cambridge Dictionary

- "Dialogue is often critical for <u>moving the plot of a story forward</u>, and can be <u>a great way of conveying key information</u> about characters and the plot." - litcharts.com

  ○ Surely dialogue **has** to move the story forwards in some way otherwise what's the point of it!

- "Monologue: a long speech by one person" - Cambridge Dictionary

- ○ I do not believe this to be true at all! For example, how do you define 'long speech'? The key attribute of a monologue is that **no-one else is present**. Long speeches in Shakespeare are often referred to as examples of monologue, but these are not monologues at all if there are other actors on stage at the time. So, in spite of what some definitions may say, monologue is <u>**not**</u> a long speech in a dialogue — nor is a poem a monologue, which is what some definitions also claim.
- "In drama, monologue is the **vocalisation** of a character's thoughts; in literature, the **verbalisation**... A monologue speaks <u>*at*</u> people, not <u>*with*</u> people." - literaryterms.net
  - ○ This last differentiation 'at' vs. 'with' is critical).

Does any of that help? Instinctively we actually know what the two forms of speech are:

DIALOGUE IS TWO OR MORE PEOPLE IN CONVERSATION WITH EACH OTHER; MONOLOGUE IS SOMEONE ESSENTIALLY TALKING TO THEMSELVES (WITH NO-ONE ELSE PRESENT)

Perhaps it's that simple.

What *isn't* so simple — and certainly not as easy as we may believe! — is the writing of <u>realistic</u> speech. The fact is that most written dialogue is *not* a true representation of how people talk. As writers we face a challenge to make our dialogue authentic, especially as in real life speech is often gibberish, incomplete sentences peppered with filler words and meaningless sounds ('like', 'so', 'um', 'er'). And when we come across writing that tries to be truly representational — *including* heavy use of dialect — what is presented to us can be really difficult to consume. I recently read a novel where one character's speech was punctuated with 'like' in almost every sentence. Whilst this may have been an accurate depiction of an abhorrent, lazy, and sadly all too prevalent contemporary linguistic trait, it made the book's reading intensely frustrating. I almost wanted to give up on it, simply because of that!

So if you are trying to be 'realistic' just be careful you don't go too far.

Also, ensure that your character's dialogue is accurate in terms of being true to the era your narrative occupies. I came across a story set in the 19th century where a character referred to being out of their 'comfort zone'. The words leapt off the page as being out of place. I checked; the first use of 'comfort zone' was in the 1970s or thereabouts. Such slips in dialogue can undermine the credibility of a narrative just as much as something that is unreadable.

This leads on to perhaps the most fundamental aspect of both dialogue and monologue: the words spoken are a key component of an individual's character, they are part of that individual's unique make-up and what defines and differentiates them. If you have worked through the chapter on character profiles I would recommend one of the questions you ask of each of your characters is "how do they speak?" — because dialogue is a perfect way to flesh-out 'character'.

Here are three examples:

~

"A single man of large fortune; four or five thousand a year. What a fine thing for our girls!"

"How so? How can it affect them?"

"My dear Mr. Bennet," replied his wife, "how can you be so tiresome! You must know that I am thinking of his marrying one of them."

"Is that his design in settling here?"

"Design! Nonsense, how can you talk so! But it is very likely that he may fall in love with one of them, and therefore you must visit him as soon as he comes."

- *Pride and Prejudice*, Jane Austen

The primary thing you notice in this wonderful exchange is that Austen barely tells you who is speaking. There is no consistent 'he said'/'she said', just that one "My dear Mr. Bennet" — not that you need much in the way of authorial interruption because in the words spoken, the tone of voice used, not only can you tell who is speaking but their words convey something of their individual personalities too.

"Would you rather put it off for a few days?" I asked.

"Oh, it isn't about that. At least —" He fumbled with a series of beginnings. "Why, I thought — why, look here, old sport, you don't make much money, do you?"

"Not very much."

This seemed to reassure him and he continued more confidently.

"I thought you didn't, if you'll pardon my — you see, I carry on a little business on the side, a little side line, if you understand. And I thought that if you don't make very much — You're selling bonds, aren't you, old sport?"

- *The Great Gatsby*, F. Scott Fitzgerald

In this snippet of dialogue you can see how close Fitzgerald manages to get to how individuals *actually* speak — and without any clumsiness. The fragmented sentences, the hesitations, are all perfectly paced; and again the language used by the two protagonists is distinctive and illuminating.

~

> "I think it's the best thing to do. But I don't want you to do it if you really don't want to."
>
> "And if I do it you'll be happy and things will be like they were and you'll love me?"
>
> "I love you now. You know I love you."
>
> "I know. But if I do it, then it will be nice again if I say things are like white elephants, and you'll like it?"
>
> "I'll love it. I love it now but I just can't think about it. You know how I get when I worry."
>
> "If I do it you won't ever worry?"
>
> "I won't worry about that because it's perfectly simple."
>
>   - *Hills Like White Elephants*, Ernest Hemingway

Here Hemingway demonstrates two other aspects of realistic dialogue: repetition, and that back-and-forth two people can have when speaking (especially in emotional moments) as if they are hitting a tennis ball over a net. On the face of it there is less differentiation in the language used (compared to the other examples above) but we do get a sense of one character being more emotionally vulnerable and insecure than the other. One trick lies in the fact that only one character is asking questions; a simple device which, in our reading, we might miss entirely even as it is having the desired effect.

These short but masterly examples are intended to give a glimpse into the world of good dialogue and how it can be used to inform character and progress the narrative. All three move the narrative forwards in some way.

It is not uncommon for writers to struggle to handle speech deftly, not only in terms of content — i.e. what's said — but how it appears on the page. How often, for example, do you see dialogue continually punctuated by "he said / she said"? In the examples above there isn't a single "said" — and only one "asked" and one "replied". This isn't to say that the use of "said" isn't valid, but rather that it's overuse can devalue the quality of the writing. In some instances, "he said / she said" simply becomes noise.

Luckily there are numerous alternatives to letting the reader know who is speaking, such as:

- tone of voice;
- the use of characters' names — "Mr. Bennett";
- underlying actions;
- describing how words are delivered — "He fumbled with a series of beginnings.";
- the influence of external forces, and so on.

The structure of dialogue as it appears on the page has also changed. Granted, the examples above are 'traditional', but these days the writer has many more options other than quotation marks to show someone is speaking:

- hyphens;
- italics;
- indentation;
- nothing at all..!

Have a play with some dialogue you have written. It is entirely possible that an unconventional layout may fit the nature of your narrative — time, place, theme etc. — more appropriately than the traditional norm.

~

Of course a number of these considerations disappear entirely when writing monologue; for example, you don't need "said" at all because there is only one person speaking. Similarly, you shouldn't interrupt the speaker's flow in any way, though if you do (by explicitly inserting action and description, for example) then you are putting yourself, your authorial presence, right in the middle of the monologue — which can cause issues e.g. loss of impact for the reader. (Though if the monologue is written for the stage, putting in directions for movement and action is an entirely different consideration.)

Without any authorial voice or second character there will be a paucity of description and so the writer of dialogue has to do more of the heavy lifting. That is to say the opportunities to elaborate which authorial intervention and interaction in dialogue give you (to infer emotion, describe feelings and past actions, define relationships etcetera) are denied the writer of monologue. This means that the *tone* and *voice* used in the monologue are critical.

Here are a couple of examples:

> I never thought I'd land up here, only I've not been sectioned and if I wanted I could walk out tomorrow, but the way I am now one place is much like another. Dad comes and sits, bit wary at first but our Maureen comes all the time. Brings her homework and does it at the bottom of the bed. I've got to like her more now than I used to. Of course, she's got no competition as Michael hasn't been near.

> I blame the therapist, Marny her name is. A doctor but just in ordinary clothes. No white coat. Lots of frizzy hair. Because I wasn't in here to begin with. I was at home. I was on tablets and it was miserable but we were managing. Only Marny has a thing about goals, recovery is a journey and all that stuff, and now that Michael has a girlfriend one stage would be if the girlfriend stopped the night.
>
> - "An Ordinary Woman", Alan Bennett

Bennett — through his *Talking Heads* series of monologues — is a master of the genre. In this example, with the woman of the title breaking the 'fourth wall' and talking so casually but directly to us through our television screens, we find out so much: about her mental state; her relationship with her children; her relationship with the medical profession (and perhaps authority more broadly); her medical history; her son's approximate age... And all in two paragraphs! This is what I meant about the writer needing to 'do the heavy lifting'. Because she has no-one to interact with, to 'bounce-off', Bennett has to have the woman impart all that information to us almost without seeming to do so.

> I was thinking of so many things he didn't know of Mulvey and Mr Stanhope and Hester and father and old captain Groves and the sailors playing all birds fly and I say stoop and washing up dishes they called it on the pier and the sentry in front of the governors house with the thing round his white helmet poor devil half roasted and the Spanish girls laughing in their shawls and their tall combs and the auctions in the morning the Greeks and the Jews and the Arabs and the devil knows who else from all the ends of Europe and Duke street and the fowl market all clucking outside Larby Sharans and the poor donkeys slipping half asleep and the vague fellows in the cloaks asleep in the shade on the steps and the big wheels of the carts of the

bulls and the old castle thousands of years old yes and those handsome Moors all in white and turbans like kings asking you to sit down in their little bit of a shop and Ronda with the old windows of the posadas

- Ulysses, James Joyce

The 'Penelope' section in *Ulysses* is, of course, unparalleled both as a sustained piece of writing and a monologue. Perhaps echoing the challenge of writing realistic dialogue, Joyce attempts to give us Molly's 'realistic thinking', an almost shotgun-like interpretation of the world, her past experiences, her present emotions. Were are told so much in this impressionistic and fragmented tapestry of thought — yet, unlike with the Bennett, Joyce leaves the interpretation to us. Without any structure or truly anchored reference points, the reader's job is to create an image of Molly by sifting through the flotsam of her thoughts. Although radically different, it is another example of the author having to do the 'heavy lifting'.

These two examples demonstrate that monologue can be written in such a way that it sits anywhere on the spectrum from cohesive and structured to totally chaotic. Hopefully they also go some way to proving that

MONOLOGUE IS NOT MERELY A ONE-PERSON DIALOGUE

If we write monologue as if a character is speaking to another person who is present but silent, there is a danger that we will write something flat and uninspiring.

THE QUESTIONS YOU NEED TO ASK YOURSELF...

So there you have it, some of the critical elements of dialogue and monologue — and a key difference between the two.

Given probably all fiction writers have, at some point, written dialogue — and so very few a true monologue — the questions you should ask yourself inevitably concern the former.

Looking back on something you have already written or a current work-in-progress, when it comes to dialogue:

Have you differentiated the speech of your characters in such a way as to make them suitably distinct — or do they 'sound' the same?

One tell-tale clue to this is that you constantly need to be using 'he said / she said' (or something similar) to differentiate between the two.

Do your characters continually refer to each other by name?

This is, of course, related to the question above; but more than that, it is a fundamental error writers make when putting dialogue together. Listen to conversations in the real world. People rarely refer to each other by name because they are looking at one another when speaking: Jack knows Jill is talking to him because she is looking at him when she does so; she doesn't need to preface or end everything she says with "Jack".

Is your characters' speech 'realistic' — and if so, is it actually readable?

You may think you've written something 'realistic' — especially if you've used dialect or those lazy filler words and sounds — but is it well done? One way to find out is to read it aloud, recording your reading if possible so that you can listen to it afterwards.

...AND THINGS TO TRY

Again for a chunk of already-written dialogue, why not take out the names (all those 'Jacks' and 'Jills') as well as all the instances of 'he said / she said' etcetera. Can you still tell who's who? Does it read like a credible dialogue between two or three people? If not, why is that? Do the characters sound the same?

In terms of making speech patterns unique to a character, have you included that question in any character profile? Or have you not thought about it at all?! Step back and define how you want your characters to speak: tone, idioms etc. Once you have done this, go back to the dialogue and lightly edit their exchanges to ensure that the dialogue conforms to your image of them. Is the encounter now more authentic?[6]

If you have never written a monologue, do so. Choose a character and write something as if they are looking into a camera and speaking directly at you. Once you have done so, assess whether or not their speech might just as easily be part of a dialogue i.e. have you done enough of the 'heavy lifting' in order to convey the information you wish to get across to the reader? Is there sufficient 'show', or too much 'tell'? If you were to introduce a second character would the speech of the first 'monologue character' hardly needed changing? If so, then you've not quite nailed a monologue style.

But whether dialogue or monologue, there is one common 'golden rule':

IF IN DOUBT, READ ALOUD

Yes, modern word processing software can 'read' your text for you, but it does so without the appropriate inflections, pauses, nuance. Nothing can beat your reading the piece, recording it as you do so, and then listening back — unless you have a friend willing to do that for you. Under those circumstances you are testing both a reader's reading, and the quality of the dialogue / monologue at the same time!

---

[6] One great example of differing tones of voice can be found in Julian Barnes' *Love, etc.*

POETRY ON THE PAGE

Where else other than the page?! Well, for a start there has been a rise in 'performance poetry' over the past few years, fuelled in part by by shifts in music. In the same way that the boundaries between poetry and prose have blurred almost to non-existence, so Rap is providing a similar bridge between poetry and music. Could you argue that Rap is poetry with a backing track? I wonder…

These fusions of styles — as well as the continued dominance of poetry as a literary genre you read from the page — pose two questions: the first is to ask what poetry *is* in this day and age, and the second seeks to understand the role of 'the page' and 'white space' in modern poetry.

SO, WHAT IS 'POETRY'?

A couple of hundred years ago this would have been an easy question to answer. There were rules after all, rules concerning rhyme and structure and metre; and poetry was a work of literature which adhered to those rules. But gradually, akin to the loosening of strictures in other art forms across the last century or two — in prose, painting, sculpture and music — poetry has become less regimented. **In the twenty-first century there really aren't any rules any more.**

But there are still definitions. Here are some (with my emphasis):

- Poetry is a literary work in which the expression of feelings and ideas is given intensity by the use of *distinctive style and rhythm* - Collins Dictionary

- So, there should be something in the style and rhythm of poetry which differentiates it from prose. We talk about 'poetic language' or something being 'prosaic', statements which are more often than not driven by the sound of the words (either when read aloud or in our heads), their 'feel', how 'concrete' or inventive images are.

- Poetry is literature that evokes a _concentrated imaginative awareness_ of experience or a _specific emotional response_ through language chosen and arranged for its _meaning, sound, and rhythm_ - Encyclopaedia Britannica

  - In addition to sound and rhythm, 'meaning' now raises it's ugly head — but again it is something which is nebulous and slippery, not concrete as in prose. In fiction a 'full moon' is probably simply that; in a poem it is likely to represent something else entirely.

  - And by 'concentrated imaginative awareness' do we mean language that has been boiled down, reduced to constituent parts a little like the chemical residue after evaporation? The original solution is perhaps represented by prose; the residue left after its reduction become the concentrated language of poetry. This is an idea supported by the following definition:

- Poetry is an art form in which human language is used for its _aesthetic qualities_ in addition to, _or instead of_, its notional and semantic content - poetry.org

  - For 'notional and semantic' read 'concrete'. Yet the concrete is vitally important in poetry too. A poem without anything concrete is likely to _sound_ 'poetic' but succumb to the wishy-washy and meaningless.

- Poetry is words strung together to form sounds, images, and ideas that might be _too complex or abstract to describe directly_ - literaryterms.net

◦ The suggestion here is that prose is somehow inadequate; there are things it can 'describe directly' (the 'concrete'), but others — 'sounds, images, and ideas' — it is unable to adequately convey because they are 'too complex or abstract'. Does that sound about right — or is it setting up poetry as being a superior form of literary effort, capable of doing more that prose? And if so, what is it that manifests the difference? Presumably 'style and rhythm' and 'imaginative awareness'…

Whatever the most accurate definition (and I doubt whether there is one suitable to fit our contemporary times) there can be little doubt that there are some works masquerading as poetry when they are no such thing — and I don't mean that they are prose. These are pieces which can neither be read on a page nor read aloud because their words have been blacked out, or covered by smudges, or are variously 'unreadable'; pieces which contain only one word continually repeated, or which do not contain any 'real' words at all. Surely one of the most fundamental roles of poetry is to communicate, to transmit something between poet and reader, to generate a feeling, to share an emotion, and provoke *a response based on the language used*. If you are unable to read something or if the words in the 'poem' are being deliberately obscured or make no sense, how are you communicating anything? The response provoked is likely to have very little to do with the words in the 'poem'.

GIMMICKRY IS INCREASINGLY BEING MISTAKEN FOR QUALITY AND APPRECIATED 'INTELLECTUALLY' BECAUSE IT IS 'DIFFERENT', NOT BECAUSE IT IS GOOD WRITING - WHICH MOST OFTEN IT IS NOT

But that's a fine line, the one between poetry and gimmickry — especially in an age when how words are presented on the page have become an intrinsic part of a poem's 'meaning'. Perhaps in some of the instances of 'gimmickry' the only place 'meaning' can be found is in its form and not in the words used (or lack of them). But if so, is that poetry? Or is it a kind of 'word collage'?

The traditional formal structures of poetry haven't gone anywhere, of course, it's simply that they are far less fashionable. Having said that, often a poet's mastery of their craft will be more evident via traditional formats.

Here are a few examples:

- Sonnet - 14 lines; historically written in iambic pentameter
    - The Italian, two stanzas of 8&6 lines, ABBAABBA CDCDCD rhyme scheme
    - The Elizabethan (or Shakespearean), stanzas of 4+4+4+2 (typically), ABAB CDCD EFEF GG rhyme
    - The Spenserian, 4+4+4+2, ABAB BCBC CDCD EE
- Sestina - 39 lines (6 stanzas of 6 lines, 1 stanza of 3)
    - The end words of the first stanza are repeated in a different order as end words in each of the subsequent five stanzas; the closing envoy contains all six words, two per line, placed in the middle and at the end of the three lines. The patterns of word repetition are as follows: 1 2 3 4 5 6 ~ 6 1 5 2 4 3 ~ 3 6 4 1 2 5 ~ 5 3 2 6 1 4 ~ 4 5 1 3 6 2 ~ 2 4 6 5 3 1 ~ the envoy (6 2) (1 4) (5 3)
- Villanelle - 19 lines (5 stanzas of 3 lines, 1 stanza of 4)
    - With the rhymes 'A' and 'B', a Villanelle's lines ('a1' & 'a2') are repeated as follows: a1.B.a2 / A.B.a1 / A.B.a2 / A.B.a1 / A.B.a2 / A.B.a1.a2 (for example, Dylan Thomas' "Do not go gentle into that good night" - which is line 'a1')
    - Often has consistent syllable count per line
- Ballad - 4-line quatrains with the rhyme ABCB

- Pantoum - a series of quatrains, with the second and fourth lines of each quatrain repeated as the first and third lines of the next. The second and fourth lines of the final stanza repeat the first and third lines of the first stanza.
- Haiku - typically, though not exclusively, 17 syllables in 3 lines (5-7-5); in traditional Japanese Haiku there are strict rules in terms of content and format!

So, what is a poem? Asked two or three centuries ago and the answer would have been a sonnet or a Sestina, a Villanelle or a Ballad...

But just being able to conform to the rules — i.e. to write a 'proper' sonnet — doesn't mean the poem will be good.

ADHERENCE TO A STANDARD POETIC FORM (OR INDEED VARIATION FROM ONE) GUARANTEES NOTHING!

Of course, at the end of the day you can choose to write whatever you like in terms of form and structure — and if it's clearly not prose or a play of some kind, you can call it poetry. No-one is going to stop you. But do you know why you are doing so, and what you are trying to achieve?

There are many ways to get your message across and demonstrate mastery of your craft without needing to delve into the ridiculousness of gimmickry.

In terms of structure, for example, you can play with traditional forms and 'bend' them to fit your subject and theme. For example:

- Write a Sonnet and don't worry about iambic pentameter or syllables per line or lines per stanza, but keep the rhyme scheme.

- In any conventional form use lots of enjambement to run on between lines, or use punctuation or space (more anon!) to break the rhythm in the middle of lines.

- Write a Sestina but vary the number of lines / repeating words e.g. 4 stanzas of 6 lines, or 5 of 4 etc.

Having said that, trying to adhere to 'the rules' can be a good way of attempting something new *and* honing your skills. When you think about it, even Rap conforms to a loose set of rules based around rhyme and rhythm / beats per line, yet few people would suggest it was a strict 'form'.

So, when it comes to today's poetry, almost anything goes — but this is a freedom which can give rise to issues relating to meaning, sound and rhythm, the very bedrock of what poetry is.

AGAINST THIS BACKDROP, HOW WORDS ARE PRESENTED ON THE PAGE HAS NEVER BEEN MORE IMPORTANT

'Look' is now something which can distinguish a poem. In some unfortunate cases, 'look' is really all there is.

There are a number of ways in which the arrangement of your words on a page can enhance meaning, rhythm, and what you are trying to achieve in your work. For example, in twenty-first century poetry 'white space' has been elevated in importance such that it is almost on a par with the language it supports. Gaps — between words, between lines — can serve as punctuation; when we see a break in a poem we instinctively pause, so if you wish to write a poem without formal punctuation, you can use white space instead, perhaps an extended space for a comma, a whole line for a full-stop. Indeed, writing a poem without punctuation and capital letters will change not only how it looks but how it 'feels' to the reader too.

The same is true of justification. Traditionally poems are left-justified, but increasingly poems can be seen with their lines centred on the page. Again this change of look will subconsciously alter a reader's perception of the words those lines contain. Some poems have lines right-justified, or a combination of left, right and centre. Increasingly, poets are also adopting longer line lengths and printing their work in landscape rather than portrait.

All of these techniques provide the modern poet with a fantastic toolset, opportunities to enhance the words they have chosen to put down on the page. And we should cautiously embrace them.

But doing so comes with some health warnings:

1 - NEVER LOSE SIGHT OF THE FACT THAT YOUR POEM STARTS AND ENDS WITH THE WORDS YOU CHOOSE. <u>YOUR WORDS MUST HAVE PRIMACY</u>

2 - IF YOU ADOPT THE USE OF LARGE WHITE SPACES OR VARIOUS LINE LAYOUTS AND TEXT JUSTIFICATIONS, HAVE A SOLID REASON FOR DOING SO – AND THAT REASON <u>MUST</u> BE TO ENHANCE MEANING, SOUND OR RHYTHM

3 - BE CAREFUL NOT TO FALL INTO THE TRAP OF PRODUCING GIMMICKRY RATHER THAN POETRY

One test you might choose to employ to ensure you are avoiding all of the above is to remove all the fancy formatting and simply read the **words** you have put down. On their own do they carry enough weight and meaning, enough poetic intent and *integrity* to justify what you are doing to them in terms of formatting?

I once read a 'poem' that was about three pages long. Ninety-five percent of all the words (and it was a piece of prose) had been struck through, redacted. When you read the words left unmolested, you discovered a rather splendid short lyrical poem. The poet had written something lovely and then chosen to bury it away for the sake of gimmickry — and in the process probably improved their chances of getting it published...

THE QUESTIONS YOU NEED TO ASK YOURSELF...

You might think that I'm going to suggest that the only question you need to ask yourself when it comes to how you present your poetry is "why vary from the traditional?" — but you'd be wrong. That's one question, certainly; but the second is "why not?"

I have seen many perfectly adequate poems given a boost by changing the way they are laid out on the page, be that removal of punctuation, or increased use of white space, or centred rather than left justified.

The key thing is to know why you are trying to do what you are doing. There is a great deal of opportunity to experiment. So you've seen a poem with long lines printed in landscape and thought you'd have a go at that. All fine and good. That's how we learn, how we find our voice. But as soon as you share a poem you are committing to it; you are saying "this is my poem, these words *in this format*". Imagine you are in a progressive open writing group where people are unafraid to ask the difficult questions. Imagine someone asks why you did something unconventional in terms of form. Do you have a proper answer to that question? Can you justify yourself? And what if they accuse you of gimmickry?

This has nothing to do with right and wrong — if anything you'll know by now that there is no 'right'! — but rather being able to support your work, your words.

Poetry is a ticklish business. Perhaps appreciation of poetry is far more subjective than for prose or playwriting. There should be an intensity in poetry, a concentration of feeling and emotion — both in terms of the poems themselves but also in the intent and investment of the poet. And perhaps in the expectation of the reader too.

...AND THINGS TO TRY

This is an area which lends itself it what might be termed 'exercises'...

- Try and write a Sonnet, Sestina, Pantoum, Haibun etc. according to their strict formal rules — then write something similar but where you allow yourself to bend those rules.

- If you don't already do so, write a poem without capitals and punctuation but use line breaks & white space as punctuation.

- Take an existing poem of your own and present it differently on the page without changing any of the words e.g. centre rather than left-justify; remove all punctuation and capitalisation; change the line lengths; play with the white space. What does this do *to the words*? Even take a poem written by someone else and present it differently on the page — perhaps Hardy or Yeats or Auden — and remove punctuation, centre the lines, add white space etc. Even change a few words if you want to...

These exercises are not about writing 'good' poetry; they are about experimenting, finding new things and ideas, having fun. More than that, they are about exploring the craft of writing poetry, and about testing yourself, seeing what you can do.

Poetry on the page is about more than just the words.

THE JOY OF EDITING

Yes, you did read that correctly: the *joy* of editing!

For far too many writers, editing is little more than a 'necessary evil', something to be galloped through in order to get to the end of one thing and thus open the door on the next — after all, the fun is in the writing isn't it, not in all that checking nonsense!

Yes. And no.

When you start your writing journey the focus is on production — poems, stories, plays — and moving from one masterpiece to the next. You tell yourself that you're interested in quality (of course you are!) but somehow not if it gets in the way of building up some kind of portfolio; after all, to be recognised as 'a writer' one has to write. And for the majority of burgeoning writers during those halcyon early days there is an intrinsic belief — and the perfect excuse! — that what we've produced *has* to be good; we wrote it, for heaven's sake!

For many people that naïve self-belief never goes away — "what can possibly be wrong with what I've written?" — and hence they never entirely lose the sense of editing being the minor partner, a waste of precious time.

But here's the thing,

EDITING IS WRITING

It just is. Period.

Consider what actually happens.

Each of us has a unique internal dictionary locked away inside our heads; a dictionary of words harvested from years of reading, listening, speaking — but probably mainly reading. If you ask the internet how many words people know, you will be told that the 'average' person has knowledge of between 20,000 to 40,000 words — though one study[7] suggested a college graduate might know 216,000. For our purposes it doesn't matter what the 'right' number may be (especially as there probably isn't one!), but let's assume that as 'a writer' we are likely to read more than the 'average person' and thus have a broader vocabulary. So let's be generous, and for the sake of argument agree our personal dictionary contains 100,000 words.

When we're **drafting** — or what we typically recognise as 'writing' — and are in that process of putting words down to build something new, what we are actually doing is rapidly and more or less <u>subconsciously</u> choosing from our 100,000 word-reservoir to arrive at a sequence which — as if by magic! — appears on the real or virtual page. Is that fair enough?

When we are **editing** *we are effectively going through the same process* — i.e. choosing words from our personal dictionaries — but are doing so <u>consciously</u>. We are asking ourselves explicit questions — for example, "what's the best word to represent 'anger' in a precise location *here* between these two other words and in this larger context?" — and then making decisions accordingly: "'hate' is too strong, 'ire' too weak"…

In drafting there is a flow, a kind of mental abandon; in editing, the process is so much more about calculation.

IT IS THE 'OTHERWORLDLINESS' IN THE UNCONSCIOUS FLOW OF DRAFTING TO WHICH WRITERS CAN BECOME ADDICTED

---

[7] *The Language Teaching Controversy* - Karl Diller, 1978

Which is great, isn't it? Exhilarating, even. Who hasn't sat back after an intense hour of writing and found themselves stunned by what they have been able to produce: the ideas, the images, the number of words. Oh, it may not happen often enough of course, but it does happen!

But here's the truth of the matter:

A DRAFT IS <u>NEVER</u> THE BEST WRITING WE CAN PRODUCE

Never. If you believe that I'm afraid you are deluding yourself.

And think about it; *very rarely will a writer let a reader see a truly untouched draft.*

So let's go back to the process.

For argument's sake, let's say that in one sitting you have drafted a 1,000 word short story. Result! What do you do next? There are a number of options:

1. Print it out and give it to friends to read, or post it on-line, *not even bothering to re-read it yourself.* In this 'truly untouched draft' there is no editing at all — I mean, why would you; after all, you wrote it and you know it must be brilliant!

2. Immediately read what you have produced, make a few minor tweaks (in fifteen minutes, the odd word or typo, a bit of punctuation amendment — "those pesky commas!") and then print or post. That's the most superficial kind of editing; a nod to the process without compromising your sense of genius.

3. Come back to your story a day later and re-read it, and then take about half-an-hour to make some more considered amendments, then print and post. Now you're putting your self-belief a little more to the test, and at least you've not merely paid lip-service to the editing process.

4. Having gone through a first edit (such as in step 3), put the story aside again and return to it a day or a week later. Go through the re-read process again. And maybe once or twice more after that. *Then* print or post. Okay, you may have undermined your notion of invincibility, but at least you've edited the thing seriously.

Now ask yourself this question: which of these four approaches — '1', '2', '3' or '4' — do you think will result in the production of the 'best' story you could have created?

Clue: if you've answered anything other than '4' go to the back of the class!

How can '4' *not* allow you to produce the best story possible?

"Ah," you may say, "but my story might lose all it's spontaneity" — yet there's so much wrong with such a complaint. Firstly, spontaneity doesn't necessarily equate to quality; and secondly, if your story possessed such energy to begin with and you believe through editing you will lose it, perhaps you may not be a very good editor/reader — and thus you need to practice editing even more!

All flippancy aside, there's a critical point here.

BEING AN EDITOR IS FIRST AND FOREMOST ABOUT BEING A READER

The first thing we do when we edit is read. Obvious isn't it? Obvious but perhaps unrecognised. As is the fact that, on taking on the mantle of a reader, it is vital that we try and read our work as a third party would, coming to it as cold as possible. We can't go into that reading with a mindset that says "I wrote this, therefore it's going to be brilliant". Indeed, there is a great deal to be said for taking the opposite approach: "I wrote this and therefore I know it's going to need some work". One of the tangental benefits of Imposter Syndrome?

Actually, I would argue that you **must** take that second approach. What is editing other than an attempt to create the best possible version of something? So why skimp? In doing so you are letting down both yourself and your work.

- "Editing is the process that involves reviewing, organizing, correcting grammar and spelling, and formatting a piece of content." - editorninja.com
  - Technically, yes; but this definition is inadequate for a piece of creative writing.
- Editing: "to alter, adapt, or refine especially to bring about conformity to a standard or to suit a particular purpose." - Merriam-Webster.com
  - Slightly better perhaps. *Conformity to a standard* would fit something like writing a Sonnet or a Villanelle; and *suit a particular purpose* begins to tease at the motivation behind writing, the 'why'.
- "Editing is when you make changes that improve the finished product." - vocabulary.com
  - Again okay; focussing on *improvement* is good to see.
- "Editing is the process of selecting and preparing written, visual, audible, or cinematic material used by a person or an entity to convey a message or information. The editing process can involve correction, condensation, organization, and many other modifications performed with an intention of producing a correct, consistent, accurate and complete piece of work." - Wikipedia
  - The most comprehensive and appropriate definition of these four. It talks about *selecting*, as in words from our internal

dictionary; it talks about *conveying a message*, because when we write something we are first and foremost trying to communicate; it covers the technicalities of making changes; and it references our ambition, to produce *a correct, consistent, accurate and complete piece of work*.

But where's the 'joy' in all of this? You still think editing is dull work; it gets in the way and stops us from doing what we really want to do.

Editing is all about mindset; mindset and experience. The only way to convert you, for you to appreciate what thorough editing can do for your work, is to experience it — not the editing itself, but the looking back on the 'before' and 'after' and recognising that what you have ended up with is better than that with which you started. It is an educational process. Part of being persuaded to the joys of editing is based on undeniable empirical evidence — "this is better than it was" — and part on belief — "when I start editing I *know* I will arrive at a better place".

Personally, I look forward to the editing process. I am far from perfect at it (my reading is not quite forensic enough, and I miss the odd typo even after multiple iterations), but I enjoy finding sentences or phrases that don't quite work, word orders that can be improved, elements that are not pulling their weight and need to either be removed or replaced.

ONE OF THE MOST IMPORTANT EDITING SKILLS TO LEARN IS NOT BEING AFRAID TO CUT THINGS OUT

Take my novella, *The Red Tie*. I edited lightly as I went along and then, once the draft was finished, I did a full edit on the screen. Then I printed out a copy of the text and edited — with a pen! — on paper.

This is really important: we read *differently* on paper compared to how we read on a screen.

Then I typed up the edits and printed the whole thing out again. The process was iterative. For *The Red Tie* there were four paper-based editing cycles.

But how do you know when to stop?

Well, the truth is that you might never stop. Ask many poets and they will tell you that a poem is never really 'finished'. Sometimes you will get bored editing, and boredom will most likely lead to misjudgements and a decline in quality; so try and stop before you get there. Sometimes you will just 'know'. There are clues however: when you find yourself changing a word back to how it was before, perhaps for the second or third time; or when you find yourself fussing over the same things. In my case it's commas. As soon as I begin fiddling uncertainly over commas I know I'm just about done.

And even if you have a nagging suspicion that the work isn't 'finished', sometimes you've just got to leave it alone.

So are you convinced about the power of editing yet?

Well here's the clincher:

EDITING MAKES YOU A BETTER WRITER

The more you edit, the better writer you become — and the less you will need to edit. It's a very virtuous relationship!

Here's an example. Many years ago, all too often I found I had written sentences that ended with the the words 'to' or 'for', the result of lazy grammar, incorrect word order. During the editing process I would try to ferret out those anomalies and correct them. I began to recognise clues as to when they would be likely to occur, clues that were present far earlier in the same sentence, for example in a particular sequence of words. As soon as I was endowed with that knowledge, I began to recognise those clues *as I was writing*, and found I could intercept the flawed sentence <u>before it was written</u>. My draft was better; my editing process lightened.

There are all sorts of weaknesses good editing can uncover — and then allow you to remediate for them during that unconscious process of drafting. Your use of 'go to' or 'catch-all' words for example, which you often throw in because you can't think of anything else at the time. Or super-long sentences. Or poorly constructed dialogues.

Editing is a whole stream of a writer's education.

And there's one more **massive** advantage in embracing editing.

EDITING MAKES YOU CARE LESS ABOUT YOUR DRAFT

That sounds counter-intuitive, I know, but bear with me.

If you accept the value to be garnered from a decent editing process, and if you realise that it's during the editing process that you really make you work shine, then *you can afford to be less precious about what you draft in the first place*. You can accept that it doesn't have to be instantly perfect because you can polish it subsequently. You don't have to agonise over the mot juste as you now have a process which allows you to to find it later. You can banish your tyrannical 'inner editor'.

Sharing the responsibility for producing your best work between drafting and editing can free your writing, depressurise it. You may find that your 'flow' is improved, that you can draft more efficiently, that your word count increases.

This isn't the same as not caring about what you are writing; it's being able to assign responsibility for quality to the correct part of the process.

No-one encapsulates this notion better than Ernest Hemingway:

"WRITE DRUNK, EDIT SOBER"

THE QUESTIONS YOU NEED TO ASK YOURSELF...

Let's start with an obvious one.

Do you edit?

And of course you are going to answer 'yes' aren't you?

So, if 'yes', do you edit enough?

You may not choose to answer 'yes' to this one — whether true or not! — but rather come back with a challenge "define 'enough'"... But there you go, wanting a 'right' answer again.

So let's put it another way.

Is the last thing you finished as good as you could have possibly made it? If you had given it one more read-through, one more edit, might it have been better?

That's an entirely different matter, isn't it? Much more specific — and fundamental. You want to be able to say no more editing was needed, that it was the best you had in you. But perhaps there's a nagging voice somewhere whispering that the truth of the matter might be different...

And you know what, right now that's okay. Your first challenge is one of recognition: recognising what editing is, the value of it, what it can do for you and your work, followed by understanding your relationship to it right now. Your *true* relationship.

If you edit to a reasonable degree and yet still find it frustrating or boring, or you can't see any material benefit from the effort, then I would suggest you examine your process for weaknesses or flaws. For example, do you only edit on-screen? If so, then you should ensure one iteration of editing is on paper when you are armed with a pen. You can't beat it!

Or perhaps you rush through it? Four iterations of editing sounds good, but if each one only takes ten minutes... For prose, 3 to 5 minutes per page on the first paper edit is probably a minimum.

So try and think about ways you might change your process to better suit the way you work and the 'type' of writer you are — you see, those four initial fundamental questions apply even here!

If you write both poetry and prose, is your approach to editing the two the same? Because most likely it shouldn't be. Poetry editing usually benefits from 'little and *very* often' (unless you've written *Paradise Lost*!), whereas prose needs longer and more sustained periods of effort.

Or at the other extreme, do you 'over edit'? Do you obsess over perfection, never happy that something is 'finished'? Under these circumstances you may need to force yourself to let things go. One way of doing this is is put work aside for longer and longer periods before coming back to it. Eventually you won't come back to the piece because you will be busy working something else.

And in terms of 'negative' editing, one common issue is when time and again you find yourself continually tweaking what you last wrote to such an extent that a) that's all you do, and b) it stops you from drafting the next part of the text. This is the tyranny of your inner editor, the voice that demands you don't carry on until you have polished to a high sheen what you've already written. This affliction often manifests itself in a lack of creative momentum, the complaint that you're "stuck". In such circumstances you have to learn to give yourself permission to produce imperfection. Remember one of the by-products of editing: learning to care less about your drafts.

BEING A GOOD EDITOR CAN MEAN KNOWING WHEN <u>NOT</u> TO EDIT TOO

...AND THINGS TO TRY

If you tackle all the questions above you should be able to form a reasonable idea of what you need to do next. Most likely it will revolve around an adjustment in your writing process i.e. when, how, and how often you edit. It may also involve a fair degree of self-discipline to stick to any revised ways of working.

But if you are stuck for ideas or simply need to go a little deeper into what editing means, perhaps try these:

- Select a piece of your own work, something you consider 'finished'. In this instance older work is better as it will be good to have a certain 'emotional distance' between you and it. Then sit down and create a revised version by going through a thorough edit (ideally on paper). This should be a decent effort, so allow yourself an aggregated time window equivalent to perhaps a minute per line for poetry, and around five minutes per page for prose. Come to the work as 'cold' as you can, accepting that the 'you' who wrote it is different from the 'you' now editing it. Compare what you come up with from this new edit against the original. Better or just different? It certainly shouldn't be exactly the same — and if an inner voice tells you that the original cannot be improved upon, then do not listen to it! This exercise can also be a great way of resurrecting work that perhaps you have always regarded as never being quite 'right'.

- If the thought of beginning by re-dissecting your own work is a little daunting, then take someone else's: perhaps a poem by Ted Hughes or Dylan Thomas, a paragraph or two from a published novel. Look at the work *as if it was yours*: what do you want to change? Can you make it 'better', overlay your own voice? Obviously this isn't about creating unique or publishable works of art — they're already there! — but rather it offers a way to sharpen your editing knife, to get experience of pruning and embellishing, and to show how it is possible to regard work as never truly 'finished'. Editing something which is 'not yours' can be a great exercise; with the words belonging to someone else you are more or less ensured of the emotional detachment from which editing can benefit.

- If you suffer from paralysis brought on by the tyrannical internal editor, try writing something really short (a piece of flash fiction or a found poem perhaps) and then as soon as you have written it — and *without* any editing — put it away and immediately start on a second. Maybe do this in timed slots. Try and complete three pieces. This exercise will force you to 'accept' your first draft because you *have* to move on. Come back to these pieces after about a week and then edit them in the same way: perhaps ten minutes on one before you put it away to work on the next. The aim here is to give yourself permission **not** to chase perfection; to discover that it's okay for work to be drafted incomplete and polished later.

Of course if all else fails you can simply reach for the bourbon and follow Hemingway's advice..!

GETTING PUBLISHED

For many getting published is the Holy Grail. It is your ambition, the pot of gold at the end of the rainbow, the only thing which allows you to rightfully claim that you are 'a writer'.

And here is the bottom line:

GETTING PUBLISHED IS EITHER REALLY HARD OR REALLY EASY; IT DEPENDS ON WHAT YOU MEAN BY 'GETTING PUBLISHED' – AND WHAT YOU WANT FROM IT

Shall we tackle this one first because there's a corollary: the fact that being 'published' doesn't necessarily make you 'a writer'.

But more of that anon.

Maybe we should go right back to the beginning, to the 'why' of your writing journey. I suspect that, even if you didn't declare the reason you wrote was to be published, that goal may have never been far from your mind. For example, if you enter your work into competitions along the way, why do you do that? Almost certainly not for the prize money! Is it for the glory of winning? Or even getting close! Or is it about recognition – a reward made even more powerful when backed-up by seeing your work in print?

Perhaps take a moment to revisit your 'why' – and then think about how you would choose to define 'getting published'. Which of the following loose definitions works for you, because in order to progress on your publishing journey you need to understand what you are aiming for.

And don't forget, publishing is only half of the handshake. Publishing implies that there is someone on the other end who is going to choose to read what you have offered. Your definition has to consider that element of the equation too.

So, is 'getting published':

- Having your books stocked in major bricks-and-mortar retailers as well as available via multiple outlets on-line?
- Perhaps having some local bookstores stock a few copies as well as having them available on-line?
- Or is having ebooks available on Amazon all you aspire to?
- Finally, maybe just having a physical book is enough and you are not interested in selling it…

The range stretches from a global physical and virtual presence, through local visibility and various scales of on-line availability, to virtual anonymity. Understanding where your ambition lies is important, because the various publishing routes open to you may or may not be compatible with your end-goal.

Getting published the hard way

The most difficult route to publishing is, unsurprisingly, the traditional one: find an agent willing to represent you, an agent who then needs to find a publisher interested in your work. This is the route that would see your work picked up by Penguin or Faber or one of the major publishing houses.

But competition is *ridiculously* fierce. Agents are inundated with queries. It is not unusual for an agent to receive between 30 and 50 unsolicited queries **per day**. Given they have to service the writers to whom they are already contracted, it is entirely possible that an agent will have only a minute or two — literally! — to skim through your carefully crafted pitch. Many will make an initial decision after just a few sentences; perhaps more will never read a single word of your precious manuscript. Writers are all too ready to blame agents for not choosing them, but <u>agents have a really tough gig</u>.

All of which means that to be successful in this channel you have to be exceptionally talented, or exceptionally persistent, or exceptionally lucky. Probably two out of the three. If the publishing gods smile on you, you will find yourself in the *very* small percentage of agent-represented writers — a percentage which runs to a number of decimal places of all writers.

So this is a *very* hard furrow to plough.

Getting published the easy way

On the other hand it is relatively easy to self-publish your work. There are multiple routes for doing so, all involving a requirement for you to format the text of your book (and the cover) and produce 'publication-ready' files. So the pre-requisite here is a certain technological competence; being able to throw together a rudimentary document in Word will, on it's own, be woefully insufficient to produce a good quality end-product. And the sad fact is that an alarmingly high proportion of writers don't seem to know how to use their word processing software beyond the absolute basics. Tabs and page breaks in Word appear beyond most people... As an editor who has to deal with the raw material submitted to me, I can testify to that!

Amazon's Kindle Direct Publishing (KDP) is 'the daddy' in the area of self-publishing, but whilst it has the advantage of being free it has the major disadvantage of tying you to the Amazon fulfilment channel; bookshops and other on-line retailers are highly unlikely to stock KDP paperbacks.

Other companies such as IngramSpark, Lulu, Affinity and the like offer services which provide you with the tools to create a book (physical and/or electronic) allied to various fulfilment methods and routes to market. A book published via IngramSpark, for example, is immediately available through multiple on-line retailers worldwide (including Amazon) as well as being available to order by bookshops through standard distribution channels.

However, unless you engage additional professionals, these are largely 'no frills' options i.e. there is no marketing to speak of, and making your book 'visible' will require further publicity work from you in terms of a book or author website, social media engagement, and so forth.

And then there are all those points in-between

Of course there are businesses which will publish your book for you — for a fee. You provide the text and they do all the work around formatting and so forth.

But this area is something of a minefield. Some companies will charge you thousands of dollars to produce your novel, after which, yes you will have something available on-line and a few physical copies yourself, but that will be about it. The dreaded 'Vanity Publishing'. I saw one site quote $1,800 for a 72-page volume of poetry. To be avoided!

Others — 'hybrid' publishers — will do something similar in terms of book production, but will charge you far less as they take on some of the 'risk' themselves, investing their own time (and possibly money) into the project. And they pay royalties too, depending on sales volumes. There are various degrees of 'frill' available depending on who you go with and how much you are prepared to pay — but as with Vanity Publishing, it is very easy to spend a great deal of money for little impact, especially in areas such as marketing. Keep in mind that only mainstream publishers have a marketing department staffed with people waiting to promote your work — something which is, of course, also in the publisher's interests.

So you can see how intertwined routes-to-market are with what you are hoping to achieve. The table below is a simplification of the relationship between the two:

	the hard way	the easy way	the rest
global physical	yes	no	depends
global on-line	yes	yes	depends
local	yes	possibly	unlikely
Amazon only	no	yes	probably not
private/'no sale'	no	an option	an option

The uncertainly indicated when it comes to 'the rest' is merely a reflection of the plethora of options available.

But what about the other half of the publishing handshake? What are your expectations in terms of readership?

Volume and reach are the primary considerations. If you desire to be read by many thousands worldwide — to be a 'best-seller' or Booker-nominated — then 'the hard way' is really your only option. There are an increasing number of Indie-published large scale success stories but these are few and far between, and to some extent depend on how you define an 'Indie Publisher'. I saw one definition which included Faber & Faber as an Indie — which I find impossible to believe!

If you have no ambition for readership other than to gift your work to a few friends and family then you will have greater flexibility in terms of how you turn your manuscript into a physical book. You could even consider taking it to a local printer and have them run off a hundred copies for you. Old school.

For the majority, our ambition lies somewhere in the middle. Yes, of course we would like to be a 'best-seller', but we're realistic enough to know that's unlikely to happen. So I suspect we'll have a rough goal: sell a few copies, a hundred copies, a thousand... Assuming you haven't been lucky enough to land an agent etc., then the simple fact is that the more copies of your work you want to sell in a packed market, the harder you are going to have to work promoting it; that means an on-line presence (website etc.), social media engagement, trying to get slots at open mics or local literary events, talks at libraries and so forth. And don't forget, some of the people with whom you are likely to be engaging in this way will be in exactly the same boat as you — so sympathetic, yes, but also your competition.

Some individuals are ridiculously successful at self-promotion: they have the personality for it, the knack to know what works, the supporting skills — and a contact list to die for! Never underestimate the value of a good mailing list. However, most writers — Imposter Syndrome notwithstanding — are unlikely to be stars of self-promotion.

So the overall message is <u>go into publishing with your eyes open</u>, not only in terms of routes to market but also outcomes. For a collection of poetry, for example, a 'best-seller' would shift about 300 copies — and in a *really* crowded market where there are thousands of 'unknown' poets, getting to fifty is a pretty big deal.

UNDERSTAND YOUR END GOAL BEFORE YOU COMMIT TO SPENDING MONEY YOU ARE UNLIKELY TO RECOUP

One aspect of your book that is really important — and which *may* make sense to invest in — is your cover. Take a look a ebooks on Amazon; based on the cover alone, it is often all too clear which have been self-published: the layout and design is poor; the image or picture used lacks any kind of novelty; and — the biggest 'tell' of all — the fonts used are hackneyed. I have seen so many self-published books using a bulk standard 'script' font on the cover. I'm sure the author has done so in order to try and make the book look sophisticated, but it doesn't. Period. My suggestion would be to avoid script and all the obvious and popular fonts — Arial, Times New Roman etc. — after all, you want your book to stand out, and in a good way!

~

And now the second — and more thorny — issue associated with publication: **that being 'published' doesn't necessarily make you 'a writer'.**

But how can that possibly be true?

It's something which clearly doesn't apply to those writers who have an agent and a publishing contract. If we go all the way back to the earlier definitions of 'a writer' — those which emphasise the professional or income-related aspects of the craft — then people who are agented and mainstream-published can clearly call themselves writers. Of course, *that doesn't imply anything in terms of quality* (though perhaps it does reflect on commerciality); nor does it follow that they are any 'better' than you. Yes, they *may* be supremely talented, but on the other hand it is just as likely that they are persistent and lucky.

"But come on," you complain waving your book in my face or pointing to a page on Amazon, "here's my proof."

A few years ago I made a sculpture of a flower using heavy-duty wire. It was designed to sit in the garden. I still have it and, yes, it's still in the garden. But I'm not a sculptor. Similarly, I once went on a painting holiday in Tuscany and produced numerous paintings, sketches, and line drawings. Even framed one or two. But I am no artist.

So it is with writing. Just because you have produced a novel — used KDP to get it out into the world where it now sits on Amazon (only available as an ebook alongside perhaps two or three million others) — doesn't mean you are a writer. It is proof that you can write, yes, and have the discipline to put thousands of words together; but that and being 'a writer' are subtly very different. I once attended a reading by an Amazon self-published author. Virtually every sentence they read began with 'He'; there was no variation or rhythm in the writing; it was monotonous. They had written something, but were they 'a writer'?

There was a famous lawman in America's 'Wild West', Wyatt Earp. Earp and his brothers were badge-wearing enforcers, the archetypal 'good guys' going after the 'bad guys' — even if the boundaries between the two were very blurred indeed. The Earps were most famous for a gunfight at the OK Corral in Tombstone, an incident which has become legend thanks to the intervention and reinterpretation of Hollywood. Wyatt Earp wrote an account of the gunfight at the OK Corral; it's an account from which a book has been created, and which — "independently published" — is available on Amazon[8]. I know; I have a copy. But the volume is poorly edited and laid out, and the whole thing not well-written at all. Wyatt Earp may have written at least part of this book, but he was not a writer.

And I daresay he had no ambitions to be one. Staying alive was most likely his primary occupation!

My point is that **being a writer is about more than 'getting published'**. In a way, getting published may not 'prove' what we would like it to — in the same way that *not* being published doesn't stop you from being considered a writer.

I know this opinion is contentious for many. There are those people who believe that 'if you write then you're a writer'; but that is not a philosophy to which I can subscribe. If I call myself 'a sculptor' that's an insult to 'real' sculptors; if I call myself 'an

---

[8] *My Fight at O.K. Corral*, Wyatt Earp, edited by H.P.Oswald (undated)

artist' or 'a photographer' then I am belittling the work of those who really can lay claim to those titles.

GETTING PUBLISHED AND BEING A WRITER ARE NOT NECESSARILY COINCIDENT

THE QUESTIONS YOU NEED TO ASK YOURSELF...

Simple really — but you may need to go all the way back to your 'why' and 'who' questions in order to re-ground yourself before you answer…

Do you want to be published?

> This one is the easiest of them all: 'yes' or 'no'. There are no other acceptable answers.

And if you do, what do you mean by 'being published'?

> Do you mean visible to the world, or invisible i.e. only for a small private clique?

> Then think about it in terms of format — paperback, hardback, ebook, audiobook, even performed plays — as well as the 'where' of publication: internet only, local bookstores, national or global, physical or virtual.

And once published, what does your readership look like?

> We touched on this when originally looking at the 'who' of your writing, but try and be specific in volume terms — both of readers and income i.e. sales. And think about how you are going to reach your readers.

Write down you answers, then scrutinise them. Does what you read resonate with the writer you want to be, the writer you would be happy to be, the writer you are happy to work at being?

Be harsh.

HAVE YOU PAINTED A SET OF 'GETTING PUBLISHED' GOALS THAT ARE REALISTIC?

There's a fair chance that you may not have done. If that's the case, circle back and have another pass at the answers. Then once you are settled on what 'getting published' means for you, take a look at the table above and see which segment you might need to occupy.

If you come to rest on *global, the hard way* then I seriously suggest you think about your answers one more time. This isn't to say that you can't be successful, but your chances are probably up there with winning your national lottery — if not worse.

Consider the 'why' of your writing, and what gives you the most joy, makes you happiest about it. Chasing the ultimate prize could easily destroy all of that. Is being realistic and content better than being over-ambitious and continually disappointed?

It's a hard school.

...AND THINGS TO TRY

If we assume that you've the writing taken care of (i.e. you have a manuscript or you are working towards one) then in relation to publication the best thing you can do is research. Along with the internet, *The Writers and Artists' Yearbook* (published annually by Bloomsbury) is a great resource.

And what should you research? Well, depending on what you are writing:

- Agents who focus on your genre;
- Publishers who publish your genre;

- Self-publishing facilitators like IngramSpark, Lulu, Affinity and the like (and yes, if you must, KDP);
- Businesses that offer publication services from editing all the way through to book production — though be careful!
- Business who offer ancillary services such as marketing and book promotion;
- What it takes to set-up an author website, a book website.

There are multiple potential partners; doing some groundwork can only be beneficial to you longer-term.

Your goal should be to arrive at a point where you can clearly see your direction of travel — and seeing it, understand your best route for getting there.

But remember, the average income for a writer is c. $7k per annum. If you get carried away, you could blow that and more on producing something that sold fifteen copies.

Like I said, it's a hard school.

SUNDRY ITEMS

PLOTTING

As far as long-form fiction is concerned, planning and plotting go hand-in-hand. It's obvious isn't it? Indeed, if you adopt the kind of planning approach outlined earlier in this book — one which leads to a raft of 'plot points' captured in a list, a spreadsheet, or written on a pile of 3x5 index cards — then the link is clear: if a plan is an attempt to say how and when you are going to complete something, then plot points are the individual elements on that journey.

However, it is also important to recognise that both planning and plotting are iterative exercises. Unless you are writing something like historical non-fiction with a set structure of one chapter per year or decade, then it is almost inevitable that there will be some movement along the way in both plan and plot. Unexpected events derail the best of plans. At the macro level this could be something external which steals away your time and has nothing to do with writing; at the micro level it could easily be that you suddenly have a fresh idea — for a character, an event etc. — which requires a change of tack: for example, you discover your A-B-C sequence has become A-B1-B2-B3-C...

And how do you plot anyway? If you are not an out-and-out 'pantser' then you will want to give yourself some structure within which to work. And what, exactly, is a 'plot'? Some definitions (with my emphasis):

- "careful foresight in *planning* a complex scheme" — Merriam-Webster.com

- "the *plan*, *scheme*, or main story of a literary or dramatic work" — dictionary.com
- "the *sequence* of events in which each event affects the next one through the principle of *cause-and-effect*" — wikipedia.com
- "the main events of a play, novel, film, or similar work, devised and presented by the writer as an *interrelated sequence*" — Oxford languages (for Google)

The relationship between plot and plan is clear: "scheme", "sequence", "cause and effect".

Given the above, one follow-on question could be to ask to what your plot is anchored, as it must have some kind of 'root' and a link between its component parts in order to work. Without such interdependence you might end up with a series of short vignettes, nothing more.

If a plot is made up of 'events' (aka 'plot points') then these must occur in relation to something physical and tangible — always assuming that your fiction is rooted in the real world! More often than not, the agents upon which these events act will be individuals, the plot being the 'story' of those characters' lives, their journey from one event to the next. Or from A to Z.

PLOT: IF 'A' HAPPENS, WHAT FOLLOWS IT? – IN ORDER FOR 'Z' TO OCCUR, WHAT MUST PRECEDE IT?

Is it any more complex than that?

Not in the linear sense, no. But what if you are filling your narrative with flashback? Or if the story is told from multiple perspectives? I would suggest that you can weave your plot points any way you choose — provided you have a very firm handle on the 'actual' linear progression from A to Z.

But if you are intertwining stories and perspectives, then a word of caution: avoid the banal. Once upon a time there was a degree of novelty in telling a story from dual perspectives (e.g. David Nicholls *One Day*) and laying out the narrative in the format 'his chapter' / 'her chapter'. Or perhaps a novel has one section set in the present day, then one in the past — and repeat. Such repetition can bore a contemporary reader; there's no joy to be had in being able to say 'I know what's coming next'…

So if you are breaking down your linear plot into some kind of interwoven format, please consider some variation. Your readers will probably thank you for it.

Prose: long- or short-form

It's a question I have been asked more often that I might have expected: "how long is a novella?", "how many words in a novel?"

That needing a right answer again…

But I think this may be more than a seeking of clarity. Rather, I wonder if such questions somehow play to our need to be definite, like ticking a box. We would much rather say "I'm writing a novel" or "I'm writing a short story" than the simpler — and so much more profound! — "I'm writing". When I can get away with it, I've stopped answering the question using numbers, preferring instead to assert that someone's prose 'will be as long as it needs to be'. You could say the same for a poem too.

And I don't really subscribe to the notion that fiction must have 'a beginning, a middle, and an end'. Why should it? Why must it conform to this stricture? Start your narrative in the middle and stay there the whole time if you want to. It's the tyranny of needing 'a story' to take the reader on a defined journey which places the shackles of neatness upon us.

Sit on a bench in a public park and just write — about the things you hear, the people you see. You are unlikely to write 'a story' (at least to begin with) but rather produce a narrative that meanders from one element to another: that dog, the children on the swings, the couple walking arm-in-arm. One or more of those might turn into a story over time, but even if they don't, the importance lies in the experience of creation.

THE JOY, OUR SATISFACTION, HAS TO BE IN THE ACT OF WRITING

In addition to convention, other drivers that lead to the compulsion to 'measure' are the corners we are painted into by competitions and the like, straitjackets we willing don in order to submit our efforts to be judged (more of competitions anon). We are told there are 'limits': 500 words, two thousand words; that we should submit twenty pages, the first 'chapter'; that this demands 'flash fiction'. All of these things — which are obviously necessary from the perspective of the requestor, the judge, the challenge itself — can actually stifle us: "I'm going to enter XYZ competition, what do I need to write? Ah yes, 368 words on the theme of pink balloons…"

Fine if that's your thing or you need a prompt to get you going, but I wonder whether you'll produce anything truly worthwhile — or perhaps pieces that are genuinely and authentically *you*.

So any internal debate you may be having in terms of long- or short-form fiction is — on one level at least — to be focussing on the wrong thing. Your work will not be 'better' if it is 70,000 words rather than 55,000; being able to label it as 'a novella' rather than 'a short story' confers nothing significant upon it.

In any event, there are many examples of recently published novels which would fail traditional tests of size and scale. They are short both in terms of the number of pages and, more importantly, the number of words. Some publishers compensate for the latter by using a smaller form factor, a larger font, more white space — but that doesn't alter the fact that many a traditionalist would regard these books as novellas.

So the message is 'don't stress about it'. Don't even ask the question. Write what you want to write and stop when it feels done — whether that's 25,000 words or 125,000. Don't tell people you are writing 'a novel', because you may end up forcing yourself to pad out something which should be much shorter — and doing so can only reduce its quality. Unless you are absolutely certain, don't tie yourself to writing a 'short story' or a 'novella'; this may force you to tie off the story when it isn't actually finished, when there is more to be said.

> WRITE WHAT YOU WANT TO WRITE; IT WILL BE AS LONG AS IT NEEDS TO BE

CRITICISM / CRITIQUING

I once asked someone what they thought made 'good' criticism, how constructive suggestions should be delivered. Their answer was "a shit sandwich". The idea is that you start by saying nice things, then confess to where you think the work could be improved, and finally wrap the whole thing up with more compliments. Softens the blow; gives the writer something positive to hang on to.

Maybe. But in my experience people can latch on to bad news like a dog with a bone.

Many of us — perhaps the vast majority — shy away from confrontation; and delivering critique which *cannot* be interpreted as personal can be particularly challenging. The result — most often seen in writing groups, I have to say — is that people refrain from criticism altogether, however well-founded and well-intentioned their comments <u>might</u> have been. Perhaps that's one of the reasons a default of "that's nice" is adopted all too readily. I have even been in groups where a writer, before sharing their work, explicitly asked **not** to receive feedback. So not interested in finding out what readers think then? Not interested in improving one's craft? So not really a writer at all, perhaps…

Before delivering a critique think about how you would want to receive feedback: 'do as you would be done to'. That should be your mantra. If you would hate someone to come at your work all guns blazing, then don't do that to others. Obviously you have to take into consideration the person who will be on the receiving end i.e. what they want, what they are capable of handling emotionally. Most writers only want praise, to be told their work is brilliant; consequently, if you can find a group of people who are prepared to give generous *and* honest feedback, stick with them like glue!

At the end of the day it is only by knowing what others think of our work that we can improve. We can't pass sentence on our own endeavours — and that includes when we think something is 'rubbish', because others may really like it.

So tread the minefield of critiquing and criticism with care; enter into it with consideration for others; but never shy away from it (giving or receiving). Integrity and honesty should be your bywords.

THE ROLE OF WRITING GROUPS & OPEN MICS

Writing is a solitary business, though there are increasing opportunities to engage in group-writing sessions: a quiet hour where people share writing time, usually virtually via Zoom or some such (though you are still writing alone, of course); or more dynamic and experimental collaborative endeavours which aim to produce work from an alchemy of different voices. But in the main we sit alone and work.

Occasionally we find we need an outlet, and this usually takes the form of either a writing group or an Open Mic. Both have value — but only if you know what you are looking for and understand what you are likely to get.

Tips when considering Writing Groups

- Decide what kind of writing group you are looking for. Do you want a group whose members provide truly constructive feedback or are you merely looking for somewhere to air your work? Do you need additional structure and a regular focus? Are you looking for stimulation via prompts and exercises?

- In many writing groups the level of feedback is often shallow and of little value. If that's what you are happy with, then fine — but it won't make you a better writer. And in groups that are critique-based, is the criticism appropriate — i.e. friendly, constructive, intelligent — or something else entirely?

- Be wary of writing groups that seem to be centred around a single individual i.e. where not everyone gets a 'fair crack of the whip' or the 'leader' is on an ego-trip. It happens!

- Some writing groups are cabals of people who just write together: you turn up and write on the spot, usually to a specific theme and challenge decided on the day. There is often little analysis. Is that what you need?

In most cases you will have to attend a writing group in order to find out whether or not it will work for you. But if the fit is not a good one, do not hesitate to jump ship; your time is valuable and being in a group that is misaligned with what you want or need may steal both your time and some of your creative impulse.

Finally, if you can't find a group that fits, consider starting one. With the advent of Zoom and the like, writing groups can now be virtual. Shape the group to your needs (most likely it will align with some others' desires too) but do not make it 'your group'; democratisation and fairness are key to the long-term health of a writing group.

Tips for Open Mics

- Open Mics are tricky. In the main they are opportunities for writers to show-off, for 'five minutes of fame': stand up, read your piece, sit down again. They can be more social gathering than literary event.

- The quality of what is shared at an Open Mic is likely to be extremely variable — and some people have no conception of just how short five minutes is! Be prepared to sit through some fairly turgid work from time-to-time. It's one of the prices you pay for having your own slot. If you are only interested in high quality writing, consider avoiding Open Mics.

- Also beware Open Mics that are over-subscribed and go on for too long. I have been to events which lasted nearly three hours; people were so desperate to read that they were prepared to wait an age for their moment to shine. Such events are almost worthless unless you've an early slot. Most people lose the will to live after about forty minutes of listening to others' work, so how much attention will they really be paying when you stand up two hours later? And what will *you* gain from the experience?

Again, your time is precious. Try out your local Open Mic — but be prepared not to go a second time if it isn't for you. This isn't disloyalty, it's self-preservation.

SOCIAL MEDIA

You either love it or hate it. Social Media is either a blessing — connecting you to other writers and, more importantly, potential readers — or a curse, a necessary evil.

And to be frank, you're either wired in such a way so as to make the best use of it or you're not; being 'present' on social media either comes easily to you or it doesn't. That's a little reductive, but broadly true.

Because of that — and because there are so many channels: Twitter/X, Instagram, TikTok, Facebook, YouTube etc. — there is no 'right answer' in terms of where and how you should engage. Personal preference is the key driver, along with the fact that you'll like the way one interface works versus another, or that there are people you know on the platform, or the content which resonates with you the most is served by one particular channel.

Sociological demographics plays a part too, as does whether or not you feel comfortable in front of a camera making short videos.

Again the message is to try out the most appealing services and find the ones that work for you in terms of the way you want to engage, the content you want to make available, and the readership and contacts you will make.

DON'T TRY AND BE PRESENT EVERYWHERE

Two warnings. The first is that not to engage in social media will, by definition, restrict your reach and limit opportunities to get your name and work in front of a potential audience. That's obvious. Secondly — and equally obvious! — social media can take over, subsume you, steal all your precious writing time. You can find yourself doing nothing but reading feeds and responding to posts. If you find you're spending all your time on-line *talking* about writing but without *doing* any actual writing, then you know you've got the balance wrong.

USE OF THE INTERNET

In theory setting up a personal website or one associated with a particular book or project is easy enough given the number of service providers in the market. But building a web presence is a little bit like self-publishing: first, you need to have a degree of technical competence in order to navigate the various website-building interfaces, and second, it is *really* easy to do a bad job. In these days of sophisticated reader expectations, nothing screams 'amateur' more than a poorly designed and unattractive website — just as with the cover of a self-published book.

> PEOPLE LOOK AT A BADLY CONCEIVED WEBSITE ONCE AND RARELY RETURN

It's the old 'first impressions' adage. But if people find the website attractive and the content interesting you are in with a chance. There are also lots of 'experts' in the market who will build your website for you. Again, something worth considering. But whether you build the site yourself or not — and assuming that it functions well, looks good etc. — the critical thing is **content**: it needs to be interesting and engaging; it needs to be relevant and contemporary; and it needs to be dynamic i.e. appropriately updated. How many times have you visited a site to find the latest post is a year old or otherwise out-of-date? Irrespective of how attractive a website might be, if when you revisit it two months later it's the same as it was before, why would you go back again?

Websites (or pages on websites) that are book-specific are almost inevitably going to be static: once the book is published what else is there to say about it other than to update it with your latest five-star review? But a personal website is an entirely different matter.

IF A BOOK SITE OR PAGE IS ABOUT A SPECIFIC PROJECT, THEN THE PERSONAL SITE IS ABOUT <u>YOU</u> AND YOUR WRITING PERSONA OR BRAND

People will visit to find out more about you, your life, what makes you tick, what you think about things — and possibly writing-related news or snippets of work-in-progress. Clearly the content has to be different to a book site/page. The key is getting the balance right. Continually telling people what you had for breakfast is going to be a turn-off — and that sort of rubbish is for Facebook or Twitter anyway, as are photographs of dogs or videos of cute cats. But regularly posting about events in your writing life, books you have read, interesting prompts or competitions you have come across and such like, is more likely to keep your readership engaged. <u>You have to be giving them something they value</u>. That's how you build a loyal following: give your readers something they can be interested in — and that's *not* your breakfast!

You need to be engaging, stimulating, authentic; a website should be an opportunity to expand your contacts — it's a marketing tool after all. And it can also give you the chance to build a sense of 'community', especially if you utilise a platform such as Substack (which can also generate a little income). But whatever platform you choose, always remember that your voice is just one of millions. People will not flock to your site just because you have created it.

"IF YOU BUILD IT THEY WILL COME" <u>DOES NOT APPLY</u>

So, if you want to be 'a writer' — and you wish to be recognised as such — then an internet presence of some kind is a key weapon in your armoury.

The Fickle World of Competitions

Not very many years ago I attended the Zoom event at which the top three prize winners in the National Poetry Competition were reading their successful entries. The chap who came second or third (I forget which) started his introduction by confessing that his winning poem had been *rejected* in **fourteen** other competitions — and now here it was, one of the best three in the land. Or at least from an entry of c.15,000.

And right there is the essential fact which underlies all such competitions, poetry or prose: the outcome is entirely subjective.

Which also suggests — by logical extension — that your average creative writing competition is essentially meaningless. Being a prize winner doesn't mean that your work is 'the best'; neither does *not* winning mean it's not 'the best'. Give the same pile of entries to an alternative judge or set of judges and I *guarantee* that the list of 'winners' will be different. Yes, most likely there will be some overlap, but an identical list of winners and short- or long-listed pieces? I don't think so. There are recognised writers — particularly poets, including those who teach poetry on courses and retreats — who enter their work into competitions and are unsuccessful far more often than we might imagine. That, in part, is one of the joys of the democratic and anonymous judging process.

NOT WINNING A COMPETITION DOESN'T MEAN THAT YOU'RE A 'BAD' WRITER

So what does all that mean for us?

Well, we like competitions don't we? Or most of us, I suspect. They are an opportunity to measure our writing against others'; they act as a gauge as to how we're doing. And let's face it, there is nothing like getting the email which congratulates you on making a short-list or winning a prize. It is the kind of positive reinforcement that can work wonders. Just as you are having doubts about what you are writing, up pops something that starts "Congratulations!" and all is right with the world again. Refuelling.

Which means that, on balance, competitions are 'a good thing' — provided you enter them 'eyes open' and in the right spirit, without expectation, recognising that they prove nothing, and that the *real* prize is the potential acknowledgement that there is some quality in what you are producing.

AND FINALLY, THE 'QUALITY' CONUNDRUM

There is one final question, 'the elephant in the room'. It is a question we either ask ourselves too often — in part thanks to Imposter Syndrome — or perhaps not often enough.

Is what I have written any good?

How are you supposed to answer that? Or *who* is supposed to do so, because surely we are disqualified from judging our own work. And perhaps most significantly in the context of this enquiry, does the quality of what I have written (or lack of quality) make me 'a writer' (or disqualify me from being one)?

It's the kind of question which will raise the hackles on the back of many necks. For some it will be taboo, one of the few questions that should *never* be asked i.e. don't talk about sex, politics or religion — nor ask whether your creative work is actually any good.

DOES YOUR WRITING NEED TO BE OF A REASONABLE STANDARD FOR YOU TO BE CONSIDERED 'A WRITER'?

What are the likely answers? These four might just about cover the major bases:

How dare you! If you write then you're a writer. Period.

> Because this is the assertion of a philosophical position — a 'belief' if you like — it is an argument which cannot be countered. Quality doesn't come into it. There is nothing you can say to dissuade those who hold this position. "If you write you're a writer. Period." is almost a direct quote from posts I have seen on Substack, Twitter/X etcetera.

Make the point about Wyatt Earp and the quality of his written work and you'll still be told he was a writer. Talk about sculpting and painting, and about how badly you do them, and you'll be told that, nevertheless, you're a sculptor and a painter too — and who knows maybe a photographer, a dancer, a fashion designer, a builder... If you like to sing but do so really badly, would these same people call you 'a singer'? I doubt it.

I'm sure you can draw-up your own list of accomplishments...

Faced with such a strident view perhaps it is best to withdraw from the quality debate gracefully, knowing there is no point entering into an argument you cannot win and your opponent cannot lose.

However, I want to suggest that there's a possibility that people are confusing the *act* of writing — which is about production — with the *merit* of that writing, and which is surely where some notion of 'quality' comes into play.

WHEN IT COMES TO QUALITY IN WRITING, ARE WE REALLY TALKING ABOUT 'MERIT'?

If you are attempting to craft a sonnet in order to convey a complex emotional feeling but all you produce is laughable doggerel, yes, you may have written something, but your work has failed to meet its goals. A tick for the act, but a cross in terms of merit.

In writing groups up and down the land, week-in and week-out, you will see people who engage in the act of writing. They produce slivers of memoir, poems about their family or nature or whatever, but for many their motivation — the 'why' they write — is predominately to pass the time, to be able to engage with like-minded people, to enjoy a hobby. Their efforts may be intended as no more than the expression of a personal memory or emotion; there is no attempt at 'universality'. Many of these people have absolutely no desire to be regarded as 'a writer'. It comes back to ambition, that initial 'why' with which we started this book. You tell me I'm a writer because I write, but what if I don't want to be 'a writer'? What then?

And it comes back to definition too. My definition of 'a writer' is undoubtedly different to those who proclaim that "if you write you're a writer"…

Quality must be a consideration, but who is the arbiter here?

Perhaps this is the response from an individual who recognises that quality plays a part; "we can't all be Jane Austen!" they might joke. Or perhaps they have sat through painful hours of Open Mics and recognise that there *is* a gap between the act of writing — producing something — and that something being 'good'.

But who is to say? Who makes the call as to whether this or that is good or bad? Where are the boundaries, the rules, the test cases?

And of course there aren't any. Indeed there can't be. You only have to think about what we have already said in relation to competitions and the totally subjective nature of 'judgement': I think Z is brilliant, you think it's rubbish. Who is correct? Both of us and neither of us, of course.

There is no arbitration. If you wanted to, you might make a case to say that 'the readers' were the only arbiters. If your books sells a million copies and mine only fifteen then surely that must mean your book is better than mine… But not really. It might be more commercial, better marketed, but of higher quality?

And what if, at that mythical Open Mic, while 95% of the audience is cringing at something being read aloud, one person is moved by it, thinks it is brilliant? What then?

WE ARE EACH ARBITERS OF QUALITY AGAINST OUR OWN STANDARDS, PREFERENCES, PECCADILLOES

Occasionally there will enough people who feel the same, where there is a critical mass of common opinion to confer 'quality' on something and someone. There will be those who dislike Shakespeare and decry his work, but the bulk of popular and academic opinion will beg to differ. Not that there is any implication here that either tribe should change their minds!

Without question., quality is a prerequisite for being a writer. There is too much poor quality writing swamping the market-place.

This is a complaint most likely to be uttered by someone who considers themselves 'a writer' — and who thinks many others who engage in the *act* of writing are not. Perhaps it is partly a defensive stance.

But the complaint is a difficult one to justify in relation to an endeavour which nowadays — thanks to self-publishing, websites and the internet, and to social media in general — is so fiercely democratic. To deny people the right to express themselves and manifest their thoughts through words and then send those words out into the void, is to touch on something far darker, something political and dangerous. This stance is answering the question about arbitration by saying "*I* know what good looks like; *I* am prepared to pass judgement; *I* am happy to disqualify your efforts"...

HISTORY IS FILLED WITH DARK PERIODS WHERE INDIVIDUALS OR GROUPS OF INDIVIDUALS HAVE SET THEMSELVES UP AS JUDGE AND JURY

And yet... Take a look at self-published novels on the Amazon Kindle store. You will find instances where — thanks to the cover alone — you might be tempted to question their merit. And if you were to pursue your investigation through to reading, I daresay you would find some books amazingly good — and some impossible to complete because they lacked structure, rhythm, rounded characters, a decent plot, creative flair etcetera.

But I've heard similar complaints against novels such as Anna Burns' *Milkman* — and *that* won the Booker Prize in 2018!

So, if you want to differentiate quality in some way — and thus also the absence of quality — we come back to arbitration and judgement, and to freedom of expression.

Does it matter? I mean, really, who cares?

Here is your 'get out of jail free card'! If it's too hard to take a position or to justify that position, or to quantify what you mean including the parameters according to which you would overlay your quality lens — and if it's frankly dangerous to assume what might be regarded as an extreme position — then why not roll-over and duck the question altogether? Keep life simple. You could just agree 'quality' is entirely subjective and therefore not even worth talking about...

Who gives a shit anyway?

Fine. But if you make that statement, just take a step back and think about it for a moment. Do you *really* not care? Logically, if you're happy with a free-for-all with an absence of judgement in terms of merit then surely you're also saying that you don't need your work assessed, you don't want someone telling you that your writing is 'good' — because if yours is 'good', then, by extrapolation, someone else's must be 'bad'. And vice versa!

"WHO CARES?" WELL, I SUSPECT THAT <u>YOU</u> DO

Don't you want all those five star reviews, all those nice comments on social media, the followers, the large numbers of sales — because aren't they all, in their own way, an affirmation of quality? Don't you want to be regarded — if by no-one other than yourself — as 'better' than the next person? Honestly? Isn't some positive differentiation important from the point of view of momentum and morale? And why do you enter those competitions if it isn't to be lauded and presented with some laurel or other?

Minefield isn't it? And all arising from a simple question as to whether or not what you have produced has any merit.

THE QUESTIONS YOU NEED TO ASK YOURSELF...

And they are all questions without any guiding answers. Or questions whose answers — individual to you — help frame your dialogue about quality, even if it's only a dialogue you might indulge internally.

- Go back to the beginning of this book and ask yourself again why you write and who you write for. What are you expecting in terms of payback for your efforts? Are your rewards in any way associated with a recognition of 'quality' or 'merit'?

- And if they are, how would you choose to define quality and merit in terms of your own output? What are your measures: a nice warm feeling when someone passes a positive comment, or the hard currency of numbers: readers, 'likes', five-star reviews, sales?

- How you you feel about the possibility of failing to achieve a target level of approbation — and indeed, what level of is acceptable? Assuming you have targets (those hard numbers!) how will you feel if you miss them? What if your average review on Amazon comes in at 3.5 stars when you were aiming for 4.5? How are you going to process that?

- Who do you trust to judge your work? Is it an amorphous mass — 'the readers' — or someone more specific?

- And how do you feel about others whose work you regard as 'sub-standard' and lacking merit?

I'm not for a moment advocating you should take any specific position, but rather that you should be reconciled to the implications of quality and your relationship to it. If you think the notion is irrelevant, then see what happens if someone tells you your work is great — or dreadful. You will care then. How can you not?

In a way 'quality' is less about the work itself than your reaction to others' assessment of it (or your view on others' work) and as such, acceptance and tolerance become the key factors. As with so many things, there is a spectrum upon which you need to find a comfortable spot to inhabit. At the one end there will be those who are supremely confident in their own work and their literary judgement and who, in consequence, pursue honesty with a brutality that is bruising for those on the wrong end of any negative finding. Does that describe you?

Or are you at the other extreme where you try to avoid all conflict, keep your judgements to yourself, and as a result offer lukewarm assessments on the 'merit' of others' work — or even take the ultra-safe position that everything has merit and therefore criticism is irrelevant?

Although most people will be somewhere in the middle, this can be a difficult tightrope to walk — which is why I suggest that examining your place on it and understanding your relationship to quality and merit (in others' efforts as well as your own) is vital.

And consider this: isn't knowing your position on quality even more important if you claim to be 'a writer'? Surely it must be. If you are telling the world that is what you are, the role to which you are laying claim, then there are responsibilities that go with the territory: as 'a writer' you must have a view, however lukewarm, on the key elements in writing's global sphere. If you are 'a writer', when reading something you do so not only as a reader but as a 'professional' too. Consciously or not, your assessment will be two-fold, an amalgam of two viewpoints.

At university I had a tutor who was a renowned Charles Dickens scholar. He also had a passion for Dick Francis thrillers. Unlikely bedfellows! The two writers gave him different rewards; he looked at them through different lenses, expecting to find different things and be rewarded in different ways. Similarly, you might read Agatha Christie, or JK Rowling, or Tom Clancy, and be thrilled by the plot and the adventure of it, yet question the writing. For each of us there are a myriad of qualities that might be weighed — qualities we look for every time we open something to read.

SO, ARE YOU A WRITER THEN?

Well if you happen to be Elif Shafak or Ella Ferrante, Graham Swift or Kasuo Ishiguro then it's safe to say you are — not that they will be reading this book! Indeed, if you are an established writer with an agent and publishing contract — if, indeed, you fit the general definition of 'a writer' with which we started this journey — then you will have your answer.

Or an answer.

Probably.

After all, you may not yet be the writer you want to be...

But for the rest of us? If you are one of the unheralded thousands — even if you have a book on Amazon and elsewhere — what's the answer?

Of course, you can't possibly expect to find a definitive conclusion here. There is no 'big reveal', no 'Ta Raa!', no fanfare, no 'right answer'.

Hopefully, as you picked your way through the preceding chapters, you will have gathered some helpful clues along the way: "that sounds like me", or "that doesn't sound like me", or "I didn't think of that". Most likely there will have been Pros and Cons, and in consequence your claim to be 'a writer' may yet be hanging in the balance.

And who is to make that call?

Certainly not me — even though if I knew both you and your work well enough I might form a view. But that's all it would be, of course. So are *you* the ultimate judge — or are we both corrupted by our various degrees of bias?

So, if not you or I, who then? Is it everyone else i.e. our 'readers'? And if so, does it take just one public and unsolicited positive review to allow you to tick the "I am a writer" box?

Over the last 180 pages or so we have been compiling evidence, and — as in any classic detective story — we have arrived at the moment when the famous detective (you, me, or someone else, it doesn't matter) takes to the floor to unravel all that evidence and declare 'whodunnit'... In theory, at least.

So, are you feeling innocent or guilty? Shall we find out?

WHAT YOU MAY HAVE BEEN ASKING YOURSELF...

Here's a high-level reprise of the major considerations which may have exercised you during your reading of this book. Think of them as a kind of 'tick list' if you want to (I quite like lists!) and in revisiting them, focus on the composite picture they build — a little like an Identikit image. Or a CV for a job interview! Does that vaguely impressionistic person staring back at you look familiar — and more importantly, do they look like a writer?

Why do you write?

Who do you write for?

What kind of writer are you?

What are you writing?

Do you have a writer 'persona' or 'a brand' — and if not, do you need one?

Do you struggle to surface originality in your writing?

Do you have 'a voice'?

Do you understand where your inspiration comes from — and are you making most of its potential sources?

Do you think you suffer from "writer's block" — and if you do, do you know why and can you see how you can rid yourself of it?

Do you suffer from Imposter Syndrome — and if you do and think it negative, can you see a way to eliminate it or turn it to your advantage?

Do you believe in your writing?

Are you a 'planner' or a 'pantser'? Do you wish to change your profile?

Do you plan? If not — and if it's relevant to your work — do you know how to plan?

If pertinent to what you write, have you ever tried producing character profiles?

Again if relevant, are your dialogues (or monologues) doing all the work they should be doing for you?

If you write poetry, have you tried to experiment in terms of format?

Do you edit — and if so, do you edit enough / properly / effectively?

Are you using editing to make you a better writer?

What is your attitude to publishing? Do you know what you want, and where are you on your publishing journey?

If writing fiction, how good are you at plotting?

How do you give / take criticism?

Do you make use of Writing Groups and Open Mics?

What is your profile like in terms of social media and internet sites?

Do you make use of competitions?

Do you see the difference between the 'act' of writing and that writing's 'merit' — and how good do you think your work actually is? And why?

Laid out like this you can see how we've covered an awful lot of ground. That's quite a composite image, I think. How did you fare? More Pros than Cons? Enough to give yourself a decent pass-mark?

And after all that self-examination, do you feel like 'a writer'? Would you land that job?

But maybe there's one final question.

If you were to ask your loved ones or those you trusted most "Would you call me a writer?" what would they say?

Simple question, binary response.

It may be as close as you'll ever get to a 'right answer'…

AFTERWORDS

As I was going through the second iteration of this book's edit it occurred to me that I really ought to answer my own questions — or "eat my own dog food", to use slangy 'business-speak'.

It's only right and proper.

So here are all the questions from the last chapter but with my answers…

Why do you write?

Mainly in order to try and make sense of the world. I see my writing as a kind of translation or examination; the patient is my life — and the lives I've observed — laid out for dissection. Hopefully most times the patient survives…

Who do you write for?

Partly my ego, I suppose; and partly for a reader — thoughtful, educated, emotionally intelligent — who might just get some satisfaction from my meanderings. (With this in mind, I think the best feedback I've ever had for my novels was "you made me cry on the subway" and "this honest exploration of human nature helped me understand myself better"[9]. Priceless.)

But in the case of this book? I'm writing it for *you* — and the 'why' of doing so is to share the experience of my journey in the hope that it might just help you on yours.

What kind of writer are you?

Largely structured and methodical, I suppose — especially when writing long-form fiction — though not fiercely

---

[9] For *At Maunston Quay* and *Once Significant Others*, respectively.

regimented. Tried that, it didn't work... Much more relaxed when it comes to poetry though.

What are you writing?

This book, a rare excursion into non-fiction. And I'm currently working through an edit of about a third of a novel to try and understand if it's worth finishing.

I'm also writing ad-hoc poetry — oh, and the odd short story.

Do you have a writer 'persona' or 'a brand' — and if not, do you need one?

I've been trying to build one, even though doing so is way outside my comfort zone. Hence my Substack, my website, my Coverstory books imprint, the poetry groups I run... There's a 'public me' I'm trying to cultivate, partly for PR purposes and partly because I enjoy the groups, the publishing.

Do you struggle to surface originality in your writing?

To a degree. I've always had a sense that there is something original (in terms of form) that I can almost reach out and touch... Almost.

Do you have 'a voice'?

Apparently so. People who know my work say they can recognise my poetry a mile away; and when it comes to prose, no matter the intention I set out with, I always seem to find myself back in the same groove — of both subject and style. I've given up fighting against these. If they're me, they're me.

Do you understand where your inspiration comes from — and are you making most of its potential sources?

I use all four channels: internal and external, active and passive. If I'm in the middle of a project I tend to focus on the internal active; if I'm scavenging for ideas (I love 'stealing' people!) then I'll plant myself in a coffee shop and open my eyes.

Do you think you suffer from "writer's block" — and if you do, do you know why and can you see how you can rid yourself of it?

No such thing! There is so much to write about, and never enough time.

Do you suffer from Imposter Syndrome — and if you do and think it negative, can you see a way to eliminate it or turn it to your advantage?

Yes, I do. But it's a question of living with it. The brand/persona things helps a little because you're forcing yourself to try and rise above it.

Do you believe in your writing?

Most of the time, yes — but not always. And more often than not that belief comes with caveats and qualifications.

Are you a 'planner' or a 'pantser'? Do you wish to change your profile?

With poetry, mainly a 'pantser' (except for my multi-year project *not the Sonnets*[10]). For fiction I often start by being a 'pantser' — especially for short stories — but for longer pieces definitely end up a 'planner'.

Do you plan? If not — and if it's relevant to your work — do you know how to plan?

Yes and yes. Mainly for fiction, but always when I'm putting a book together, irrespective of genre.

---

[10] *not the Sonnets*, Ian Gouge, Coverstory books, 2023

If pertinent to what you write, have you ever tried producing character profiles?

> I started a few years ago and now I'm a disciple of them; they're invaluable!

Again if relevant, are your dialogues (or monologues) doing all the work they should be doing for you?

> Tricky one. I suspect not as much as they could be. Always an area to improve.

If you write poetry, have you tried to experiment in terms of format?

> I tend to prefer unpunctuated free verse with use of space to provide rhythm. Very occasionally I'll write something formal. And I despise gimmickry with a passion!

Do you edit — and if so, do you edit enough / properly / effectively?

> Better than I ever did; full-length fiction especially. Up to six rounds of editing. Poetry I tend to tinker with over an extended period.
>
> But I'm not a forensic reader, so occasionally miss the odd typo... It's a weakness — but I've stopped beating myself up over it.

Are you using editing to make you a better writer?

> I think it has helped, yes.

What is your attitude to publishing? Do you know what you want, and where are you on your publishing journey?

> I know where I'd like to get to; I've had the experience of having three works of non-fiction 'properly' published. But I'm happy being an independent too. Reaching out to others is a key part of my 'why' and 'who', and that's one of the reasons I set-up Coverstory books.

If writing fiction, how good are you at plotting?

Okay I guess — but then I don't tend to write 'plot-heavy' stories, so it's perhaps less of a consideration for me.

How do you give / take criticism?

Thanks to age and experience, I'm better at taking it than I used to be — though I can still be riled occasionally.

And giving? Cautious, I suppose — but occasionally reckless when I get heated. It depends on who is on the receiving end, what they're looking for, and what they're able to take. More than once I've avoided telling someone what I really think about their work because it would be crushing to them. So I try and put the person first. Isn't that the right way round?

Do you make use of Writing Groups and Open Mics?

Writing Groups are tricky. I no longer engage in those where I get no benefit. My Derby Stanza group is brilliant because they're honest, intelligent, good writers, and we trust each other implicitly. The benefit of many years working together.

And Open Mics? Sometimes — but they can be soul destroying…

What is your profile like in terms of social media and internet sites?

I have three websites (two of my own and one for Coverstory books) and Twitter/X and Instagram accounts I rarely use. My Substack is now my main vehicle.

There's so much rubbish on Twitter/X and Instagram and the like. And so much spleen. I gave up Facebook because of that.

Do you make use of competitions?

Yes — but these days with no expectation of winning. It's safer that way!

Do you see the difference between the 'act' of writing and that writing's 'merit' — and how good do you think your work actually is? And why?

> In my mind there is clearly a difference. If you sang but were tone deaf you would perform the act of singing but do so with little merit. Similarly, I do not accept that the 'act' of writing guarantees anything, either quality or being 'a writer' (at least not by my definition). Quality/merit *has* to play a part.
>
> And my own work? Some of it is pretty decent. How do I know? Comments made by people in book reviews, in groups, even in Open Mics! And, I confess, the odd boost from competitions — including winning a short story competition in 2022, and being one of four nominees out of an entry of 2,800+ for a 2024 award. (Yes, I know I said competitions were essentially meaningless…!)

If you were to ask your loved ones or those you trusted most "Would you call me a writer?" what would they say?

> I think they would say 'yes'. Indeed, I have been introduced to new acquaintances as 'a writer'. Where appropriate, that's what I say under 'profession' when filling-in forms. And it's now what I do. I have no other 'job', nothing that could be considered work which isn't writing-related.

Is all of that enough? Does it matter? Do you even care?

Those are my honest answers, and the colours I will nail to the mast.

"So, you think you're a Writer?" — you tell me…

ACKNOWLEDGEMENTS

This book as been made possible thanks to the dozens of writers I have met and spoken with over the years, especially those I have mentored at writers' retreats and worked with at various writing groups. These individuals have built upon foundations laid by the exceptional tutors and my fellow students during my literary eduction at the University of Southampton.

I am also indebted to the authors of the many hundreds of books I have read — books of various styles, types and genres, written across many centuries — all of whom have made an invaluable, if largely invisible, contribution. More visible are the contributions made by the various websites and dictionaries used and quoted throughout this work. Particular thanks goes to the compound knowledge provided by Wikipedia, a valuable resource to which I heartily encourage you to offer a modicum of financial support.

Inevitably I am also grateful for the support of my family, especially Sarah who supported my decision to give up a formal career for this self-indulgent and precarious occupation.

And, somewhat bizarrely, I am grateful to the many hundreds of thousands of words I have written during my career; words — and associated processes — which have hopefully taught me what works and, perhaps more importantly, what doesn't.

It is to all those words — whether spoken, read, written, or even yet-to-be-written — and to all the people who will hopefully consume them, that this book is dedicated.

www.ingramcontent.com/pod-product-compliance
Lightning Source LLC
Chambersburg PA
CBHW070733020526
44118CB00035B/1301